the **EMPTY** bag

Non-Stop, No-Prop
Adventure-Based Activities
for Community Building

by

Dick Hammond and
Chris Cavert, M.S.

FUNdoing Publications

To our wives, Lura & Susana, with all our love!

We are indebted to our wonderful editorial partners, Susana Acosta-Cavert, Debby Short, and Brian Brolin - Thank you!!

Cover by Chris Cavert & Isaac King
Cover Graphics by Isaac King, www.greydreamer.com
Photos by Chris Cavert, Susana Acosta-Cavert & Dick Hammond

Both authors are available for EMPTY bag workshops. See the Trainings page at : www.**fundoing**.com

Disclaimer: The authors and **FUN**doing Publications are not responsible for the misuse of the activities in this book. Also, this book does not replace proper training for the use of adventure-based activities.

For additional information and to purchase copies of
the EMPTY bag, and other publications, visit
FUNdoing Publications
info@fundoing.com
www.fundoing.com

Manufactured in the United States of America
Copyright ©, 2003 by Dick Hammond & Chris Cavert
ISBN# 0-9746442-1-8

Contents

Introduction & Other Helpful Info

First we want to thank you for picking up this book (even if you do put it back down). Our purpose in putting this book together was to capture and recapture many of our favorite propless activities that have been proven to be both helpful and fun during our Adventure-Based Activity programs. Many of the activities have been shared by a variety of people. (We are truly greatful to Karl Rohnke, Sam Sikes, Mike Spiller, and Jim Cain for their additions to this book and their spirit of adventure.) Some activities have been adapted along the way from their original form to meet the programming needs of facilitators. We have done our best to give credit where credit is due. (If we have made an error in this process, please let us know.) There is also a good mix of, what we hope will be, new activities to satisfy even the most experienced activity programmer.

We will suggest that these activities work well with groups of 12 to 25 participants ages 12 and older (more specific details will be presented within each activity). HOWEVER, please know that this is written on paper - not carved into stone. Creative adaptation can go a long way to fit the needs of your group.

Also, please realize, our intention is to document activities we have learned to know in our own ways and bring them to others who help people and communities grow. We thank all of you for your dedication to the Adventure-Based Activity forum. May you live well and have fun doing it!

Dick Hammond
Chris Cavert

In the Spirit:
Adventure-Based Activity Programming

The Empty Bag activities are shared within the spirit of Adventure-Based Activity methods. Deriving from the field of Adventure Education, adventure-based activities are used as a tool to bring about knowledge - knowledge of self and community. This knowledge is actively pursued by reflecting - sometimes before, sometimes during, and most often after the activity. The information (or knowledge) gathered in this process can then be used to affect the future of the self and community in positive ways - learned behaviors that can benefit everyone involved.

The difference between recreational and adventure-based activities is the reflection piece. Recreational activities can enhance health, happiness, social interaction, and community. Adventure-based programming promotes the same benefits but is specifically used to accelerate, by reflection, the information, knowledge, and learning of pro-social interaction - positive behaviors. It is in this spirit that we intend for these activities to be used.

It is not our intention here to go into much more detail (a little bit more below) about our personal methodologies around experiential education and adventure-based activity programming. However, we do recommend (if you have not already done so) that you explore some of the books listed in the Resource Information section. We also highly recommend that you seek some level of training around adventure-based facilitation (suggestions listed in the Resource section as well).

Here's a "bit" more personal methodology we would like to share (so we can sleep better). **Safety, Safety, Safety!** The number one responsibility of the adventure-based activity facilitator is to keep her or his group emotionally and physically safe. For the reflection process to work, participants must feel safe enough, both emotionally and physically, to take the risks necessary to explore new ideas and behaviors without the fear of rejection, embarrassment, or physical harm. Every publication we have read within the adventure-based activity field has emphasized the importance of SAFE programming and implementation. Again, we recommend that you explore some of the books listed in the Resource section.

Closely related to the safety methodology is the concept of choice. One of the strongest components of any adventure-based program is the participants' right to choose his or her level of participation - no one, at any point, is ever forced to participate in a way that takes them too far out of their comfort zone. There are always several levels of participation to choose from for each activity, from simple and mindful observation to complete physical interaction - it is up to the participant to choose. And, it is up to the facilitator (and the group) to offer and support choice. This choice concept is of course easier said than done. Through training, reading, and experience it becomes clear why it is so important.

Finally, we strongly advocate that you understand, through training and reading, how to use proper spotting technique with regards to certain adventure-based activities. There are some activities in this book that require mindful and physical spotting to make them physically safer. We do include helpful spotting hints for the necessary activities, however, reading alone will not substitute for "hands-in" experience. We can not mention it enough (but this will be the last time, promise). Attend some training that will give you the practice and information you need to be a safe and mindful facilitator!

To recap the "bits." Reflecting on the activities will help to accelerate the pro-social learning curve. Keeping the program safe, both emotionally (enhanced through choice) and physically (supported with spotting) will lead to a productive and enjoyable time for both the participants and the facilitator(s).

Reading this Book

We have divided the activities into helpful sections. The first, Frontloaders & Processing, include activities that can be used throughout a program - interjected before, during and/or after group activities. The next four sections, Ice-Breakers & Warm-Ups, Cooperation & Communication, Trust & Support Building, and Challenge & Problem Solving follow a suggested progression. The progression might be considered as less demanding (both emotionally and physically) to more demanding. (There are several progression theories out there - this one works for us.) Within each of these four sections we have tried, as well, to list the activities in a less to more demanding order - keeping in mind this is very relative to the groups you will encounter. The sixth section, Closings, are activities that can be used to wrap up a program day or even a block of activities within the day. The final section, Fun Filled Games, is a collection of activities with a competitive nature. We like to use these activites to present healthy competitive skills - how to compete and have fun doing it.

Most activities listed in the sections will follow the format of, Title and needs (mostly space considerations), Process, and Variations (not every activity will have variations). Some activities will include **WARNING** (for safety issues) and **Notes** (for facilitation suggestions). We have tried to include the important information without getting too wordy. You are welcome to add, change, and/or rearrange what you need to meet your objectives.

At the end of this book you will also find a couple useful Appendices. The first contains Challenge Energizers. These are quick and lively group challenges that can be used to charge up the group or fill some time during transitions. We also like to use these Energizers after one of those activities that doesn't quite work out the way we would like. Familiarize yourself with these Energizers so you can throw them in when needed or have this book handy to pull out and choose from the list.

The second Appendix includes Lateral Challenge Riddles - those short stories that are solved by answering Yes or No questions. One of the ways we like to use these challenges is to have someone in the group choose a number (from 1 to 30) then read the associated Riddle. Another way is to choose a few Riddles to present when it is appropriate to do so. Some of the Riddles have some interesting topical issues a facilitator could build on after the answer is discovered.

Resource Information concludes the book. There you will find reference information used to credit contributors, recommended readings, and training providers. There is also additional information about the authors - how to contact them and access their trainings and other publications.

We sure hope you find this book useful to your adventure-based programming needs. Any feedback is truly welcome.

We truly thank you for your interest.

Dick Hammond
Chris Cavert

BIG Thanks

We want to thank all our wonderful friends - Katie, Aaron, Judy, Sharmon, Lisa, Janice, Jennifer J., Terry, David, Karinina, Sierra, RB, Ron, Kerynne, John, Rachel, Jennifer B., Debby, and the ACCT and NCCPS workshop participants - for letting us take pictures of their beautiful faces. Thanks for the smiles!

Frontloaders & Processing

The activities in this section are intended to help stimulate thoughts, ideas, questions, and possible insights on what is about to happen, what is happening or what did happen during an activity or program day. Once you know these activities you can use them whenever and wherever they seem to fit. You can find more of these types of activities in some of the books listed in the Resource section. We also recommend that you read (if you haven't done so yet) *Processing the Adventure Experience*, second edition, by Luckner & Nadler for more about the methodology of processing.

Digital Contract (variation of the Five Finger Contract shared by Laurie Frank) No special space requirements. You can present this one to any number of people – takes 15 to 25 minutes.

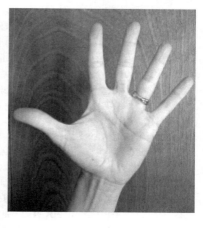

Process: Traditionally we tend to ask our groups to follow some very important guidelines/expectations as they play and learn together. If anyone is then unable to follow these guidelines we will stop the action and explore the factors that are preventing us from doing so. The Digital Contract is a tool we have been able to use to weave our program expectations into an auditory as well as a visual presentation. The visual, using the fingers of the hand, can then be used throughout the program as a reminder.

Introduce the concept by holding up one hand and spreading out your fingers (we're going to include the thumb as a finger here for those of you who consider the thumb a thumb and not a finger!?) Take one finger at a time and give the group something to remember with each finger:

The Little Finger – This finger is the smallest on our hand, it can easily be hurt. We want to avoid, "hurt" as much as possible. You might have to spell out what you expect or ideally ask the group what they expect. You could help by asking, "What kinds of hurt are there (physical and mental)? What can we do to avoid being hurt? What can we do to be safe?"

The Ring Finger – This finger stands for commitment. What is commitment? (You might need to help define this for some groups.) We are going to ask you to commit yourself to participating with the group in some way. Participation takes on many forms. (You can tie this into your choice of methodology if you want to use those words.) The least we will ask you to do is stay with the group (for safety and responsibility reasons), give your best effort whenever you can, and help the group members whenever possible. Together we can accomplish a lot.

The Middle Finger – (Avoid slinging out this finger during your explanation. Keep all your fingers up in the air as you work through them. Just a suggestion.) What is this finger often used for? (Most children know way to early what this is for, however, some don't. You will need to decide if this is something you want to teach or just move with the concept.) We are going to ask you not to use "put- downs" during our time together. We also ask that you *respect* (another concept you might explore together) yourself and others. What is important about respect? Why do we want to avoid put-downs? What will be a better way to communicate?

The Index Finger or Pointer Finger – This finger will remind us of our "Response-Ability" within the group. We want to encourage you to use your ability to respond by giving feedback to others and reflecting on the experience for yourself and how the experience will be able to benefit you and the group in the future.

You are the only one who will know how you feel. If you are willing to share your experiences, good and bad, we can become a little closer together and understand what each of our needs will be. Why is it important to get to know each other better?

The Thumb – This finger is for the "thumbs-up" encouragement we would like you to share with the group. What is important about encouragement? How can it benefit our group? What are some examples of encouragement? When can we use it?

Using these visual cues throughout a program can help you remind your participants of the expectations we have. You and the group can define each finger to fit your specific needs, but don't get too wordy or your participants might easily forget what you expect of them. After we set this process up we like to have the participants take their reminders (their hand) and turn to shake the hands of those around them to "seal" their contract with one another.

The Chicken Game It is best to have enough room for the group to make a VERY large circle for the demonstration – but you can adapt if you don't have the room. Works well with 10 to 25 players for 10 to 20 minutes.

Process: Circles are a very important aspect of communicating with each other within a group. However, circling up a group can often be one of the most challenging activities you will ever attempt. Making circles into a game can change the dynamics completely. Before you play The Chicken Game (not the Chicken Dance) you will need to demonstrate the skills (that would be circles).

The **Chicken Soup** circle involves all players standing with arms

13

straight down at their sides, close enough together so the arms are touching each other as if they were Velcroed together (often referred to as a Velcro circle). Have the group get into Chicken Soup.Let me interject here with another skill. Only the skilled "circlers" get their circles round the first time – so don't feel bad. When you ask the group to adjust the shape they made into a circle give them permission to "Cluck, Cluck, Cluck" their way into position (most groups find it fun, really!). Okay, on with more circles.

The **Double Chicken Wing** is performed with both arms in winged fashion – hands on hips, arms bent at the elbows. Players move to touch elbow-to-elbow all the way around – "Cluck, Cluck, Cluck."

The **Single Chicken Wing** (Right or Left. If you call, "right" it will be, "Single Chicken Wing Right" if it's left, it's, "Single Chicken Wing Left."), will require players to put one hand on their hip bent at the elbow. This represents a little chicken wing – we like to flap the wing around a bit for fun as we play (chicken noises work well for some groups too!). To form this circle, players sort of work their way around each other until everybody's Chicken Wing is touching the player next to them.

Then there's the **Flying Chicken** (as we say, "Chickens do fly, just not very far.") You have probably guessed it already! Finger tips to finger tips all the way around. This is the circle that requires the most room. If your space is limited, have them make multiple circles within circles or just do the best Flying Chicken circle possible.

Chicken Dumplings requires each player to find their own "personal space." This would be where everyone finds a place in the room or boundary where they have enough room to move their arms around (safely) without touching anyone else.

Since we've started playing The Chicken Game there have been other variations people have suggested like, "Chicken

Salad," "Boneless Chicken" and "Chicken Sandwich" – we're sure you can conjure up the visuals on these. Feel free to add other formations if you believe you will need them during your program. We also need to teach the, "Mingle" skill for this activity. The Mingle is a great filler and addition to many games. Mingling involves players walking around shaking hands and saying, "Hello" to each other (nice social skill). If the group is still getting to know each other there would be, "Hello, I'm Chris," with a response of, "Hello, I'm Susana." The two break off to Mingle with others. If the players know each other, it might go like this, "Hello Susana," "Hello Chris!" then Mingle on.

Okay, now we're ready to play. As the group is gathered around you, indicate the different types of circles you will be using for the game – out of the ones you have already practiced. Then, explain Mingling and do a little practice. When the players under-stand Mingling, have them stop for the final directions. When you call out, "Mingle" the group will do just that – Mingle. At some point during the Mingle you will call out a circle formation – "Chicken Soup!" The group, as quickly and care-fully as possible, must get into that circle formation. When the circle is made, call, "Mingle" again, and the group blends and mingles until the next circle is called – practice all the circle types at least once (the Boneless Chicken is fun to throw in there).

Once the players know the formations you can use them throughout your program to get into the appropriate size circles for your activities. You can also just play The Chicken Game as an energizer. **Note:** Be patient when you first try this one. If you have real young players it will take a while to get the circle you're looking for. Make sure you get the players to help each other out – that's what this is all about, right? Besides, delegation is a skill too!

Neat Names (also referred to as Ropes Course Names) You need enough room to make a circle with your group. Plays well with 8 to 25 for 15 to 25 minutes.

Process: At the beginning of our programs we like to circle up the players (Single Chicken Wing to the Right works well. See The Chicken Game for details) and come up with Neat Names they can use during the day. We challenge each player to choose an adjective or verb that would go with their first or last name. The word, we suggest, should either rhyme or start with the first letter of the name used. Dick's Neat Name has been "Dizzy" and Chris' has been "Crispy." So, as the facilitator you can move around the inside of the circle pointing at players and asking them for their Neat Name, "Magnificent Mary." Make sure the group hears the name and then have them say, "Hello Magnificent Mary" then on to the next, "Powerful Pete." You also might want to go back and review names if there is a large group of players to remember. It is okay for a player to pass if they can't think of a name. We have also let other players make suggestions – making sure the names are not disrespectful in any way (bring up the Digital Contract if needed). After a few more players share make sure you return to the passer to get his or her Neat Name. We like to use the names throughout the day. It helps us to practice and remember names. It also seems to add some fun energy to the environment. **Variations:** There are times when we might have to split a larger group into two or more groups – working around in stations. After Neat Names we might have the group come up with a "Group" name and a cheer that goes with it. This help us to identify and call our groups together after breaks – the cheers are great energizers.

Grading (variation of Scaling or Ranking from, *Reflective Learning)* No special space requirements. Plays well with up to 15 in a group (multiple groups can play) for 15 to 20 minutes.

Process: After an experience, ask the group members specific questions related to some behavior within the group or themselves during the last activity that they would be able to "grade." For example, what grade would you give the group for verbal communication? Or, "What grade would you give yourself for listening?" After some quite reflection ask for a show of hands for each grade – A, B, C, D, F. If you believe the group members can go a bit further with this process you could ask someone who gave a "C" grade, "What would it take for this group to get a "B" from you?" Going up just one grade represents incremental goal setting. You could also ask someone, "What qualities lead you to give an "A" grade?" The hope is that this feedback can help improve performance in the future. **Note:** Grading does not have the best reputation. This process might open the door to some dialogue on the topic. **Variations:** In the book, *Reflective Learning* the process is set up with a number ranking, 1 through 5 – 5 being the best. In this way participants can hold up a number on their hand at the same time. You could put like numbers together (if it's pretty evenly dispersed) and have them discuss positives and improvements to share with the group, or ask certain players how the group could achieve the next highest number.

Name Recognition No special space requirements. Works well with up to 15 in a group for 20 to 25 minutes – create multiple groups if needed.

Process: Participants are asked to use the letters in their name to answer a question or give feedback to a situation. You can limit them to just their first, middle or last names or let them use any letters from their full name. For example, I might ask, "How was the energy in that last activity?" Sue might answer, "Surprisingly upbeat." **Variations:** You could limit communication during an activity by allowing the players to only use words that start with letters from their name.

"If you don't know where you're going.....
you don't know where you're going!"

Ice-Breakers & Warm-Ups

Ice-Breakers & Warm-Ups are generally done at the beginning of a program day - but they can be used any time they seem to fit. We consider Ice-Breakers to be activities that involve learning names and qualities of the players in the group. Warm-Ups tend to have less talking and more body movement, enough to get the muscles loose and ready to go for the adventures of the day - we must not forget that the brain is a muscle too. We strongly urge you to learn everyone's name as soon as you can (if this challenge is reasonable). Names can be learned if one intends to do so!

Birthday Line-Up You'll need enough space to create a large circle with your group. Works well with 10 to 25 players for 20 to 30 minutes.

Process: Ask everyone in your group to create a Double Chicken Wing circle (see The Chicken Game in Frontloaders) and link elbows – each player links up with the player to their left and right. The challenge is to, WITHOUT TALKING or removing anything from their pockets (no pens, driver license, etc.) get into Birthday order – month and day only. There must never be a complete break in the circle during the process. This means that if a player needs to move to a different position she must first connect together the players to her left and her right. The moving player must then stay in contact with the circle during her movement to the new position. If the circle is broken at any time all players are asked to, "Freeze!" until the circle is repaired, then the action can continue. If the circle breaks much too often you might stop the group to find out why this is happening and how they can prevent it from happening again – issues of following the rules can be discussed. Celebrate their success when complete. If the energy is there move into some....

Variations: Have the group circle up into, Alphabetical Order by first, middle or last names, or from smallest to largest size of their favorite animal (you could even have them do this by using only the animal sounds), or by numerical order of the sum of their telephone number, or by distance they live from the program site, or another fun order – Shoe size, memorable historical event, Books in the bible, height, etc.

Ripples (shared by Mike Spiller) You'll need enough room for a large circle. Works well with 10 to 25 players for 10 to 15 minutes.

Process: This is a nice muscle warm-up. Create a big circle so everyone can see each other. One person is chosen to start the action and makes a motion like bending down to touch his toes. As this first person is bending down, the player to his right follows the same motion, and then the third to the right follows and so on (yes, like the wave) all the way around the circle. Once this motion gets around (players hold this position until…), the second person (the player to the right of the person who started) in the circle starts a new motion that is passed on around. Go down the line a few players to warm everyone up. (It might me helpful with some groups if the group leader stood behind and cued the next person to start the next motion). With younger groups, it might be helpful for the leader to continue to make the motions – sort of slow motion movement so there is always some movement going on around the circle. **Variations:** I've presented this same process with locomotor movements – I call this "skipples." The first player starts by moving, let's say skips, to the right along the inside of the circle next to the other players. The person to the right follows behind the first the third player behind the second and so on – all skipping of course. The first player stops at her original position in the circle, the second in his position and so on. All players continue to skip around the inside of the circle until they return to their original position. When every player is back the second player (the one standing to the right of the first player) starts a movement around the inside of the circle. Do a few skipples and then a few ripples and so on for a nice warm-up.

That Person Over There You'll need some good mingle space. Works well with 10 to 25 for 12 to 15 minutes.

Process: Gather your group together in a large circle. When you say "GO" (or any other Word Of The Day) each player should go introduce themselves to another player in the group – shake hands, say your names – make sure you emphasize that they should REALLY learn the person's name. Then, each player goes off to find a player they haven't met yet. (We have players raise their hands up when they don't have a partner and look for someone else doing the same and get together.) Greet this new person (remember the name) and introduce yourself (both players do so). Now, one at a time each player will point out the last person they met – the last person they shook hands with. The pairs may need to move around to find that person. After both players point out "that person over there" they go off to find another player they have not met yet - introducing themselves and then pointing out the last person they met. Continue as long as the energy is good. **Variations:** If (only if, because this is a no-prop book) you are using name tags, have players fill out a tag with their name on it but don't put it on yet. Go into the activity and after you meet someone exchange tags. Every player will always point out "that person over there" whose name is on the tag. At the end of the activity everyone is asked to stand to the right of the person on the tag they are holding. After everyone is in a circle, players return the tag to the "right" ful owner.

Jump Around (shared by Mike Spiller) No special space requirements. Plays well with 4 to 25 for 12 to 20 minutes.

Process: This is a nice one to warm-up the muscles. Split your large group into smaller groups of 4 to 5 players. Give all the groups a number (Mike likes 11). Each group will then work independently to try and attain that number. They do this by counting to 3 together, on 3 each player presents (shoots) a number of (from 0 to 5) fingers (using only one hand of course) out into the center of his or her group. The fingers out (we'll count the thumb as a finger too) within the small group are counted. If they add up to 11 (in Mike's game) that group is allowed to stop the action and watch the other groups get to their number. If the fingers do not add up to 11, let's say it's 9, the small group must jump up and down together 9 times (some groups do this with arms around each others shoulders). After jumping they count off to 3 again for another shoot of fingers. The added challenge to this activity is that you ask the groups not to do any planning that might "add" to their success. **Variations:** After a few groups have attained their number and are watching the action, call, "Mingle!" – learned in The Chicken Game. When this is called players walk around and shake hands with other players exchanging pleasantries such as names, how's it goings and so forth. Then the facilitator calls a out a group size, like 4 to 5 or 5 to 6 players.

Participants get into new small groups of that size. When everyone is in a group call out a number the groups can "shoot" for and jump around. Another idea if you have a drawing board of some sort (if props are around, why not?). Write out a series of numbers on the board that each group could attain. Give a time limit to see how far each group can get through the series of numbers before time runs out – again, without any planning.

Toe-2-Toe, Palm-2-Palm, Cheek-2-Cheek

You'll need a nice size open area. Plays well with 2 to 24 players (even numbers is best, however, this can work with a group of three if needed) for 25 to 35 minutes.

Process: This activity demands a bit of physical muscle movement and stress. We like to warm-up participants with other simple stretches like in Ripples and/or easy muscle movements like in Jump Around before we do this one. Each player will need a partner (have them introduce themselves if they don't already know each other). We will always demonstrate each physical action before the players perform it – either using a participant to help one of us or another facilitator if

available. First there is **Toe-2-Toe:** Facing your partner, stand toe to toe. Grab each others wrists and SLOWLY lean back into a balanced position until both partners' elbows are extended (arms are straight). Then each pair is challenged to squat down together (not beyond comfort level) and then stand back up without losing their balance.

23

Repeat if desired to attain a nice flow of squat to stand. Give that person a "high five", thank them for being your partner and go find another partner (size, most often, does not really matter). Have each player introduce themselves to their new partner and perform "toe-2-toe" with their new partner.

Palm-2-Palm is the next challenge. Partners face each other about three to four feet apart and place their palms together (do not allow them to interlock fingers). Then challenge each pair to slowly lean forward, bending at the elbows keeping their bodies straight, until their foreheads touch and then press with the hands to stand back upright. Increase the challenge by asking players to scoot their feet back a "baby step" and repeat touching foreheads and then standing back up (or making a step towards the center before standing if needed). Have them keep scooting back each time for a bigger and bigger lean – looking for the "mean lean." After each pair has reached their challenge limit have

each player give their partner a "high five", thank them for being their partner and go find another partner. New partners introduce themselves to each other. Ask each pair to perform "palm-2-palm." Then demonstrate, **Cheek-2-Cheek:** Partners stand back-to-back (yes, those cheeks) and then scoot their feet forward until the pair is leaning against each other like an "A" frame– heals at least two feet apart. The player's arms and hands are down by their sides.

Pairs are allowed to press hands together but do not let them link elbows. The challenge is to squat down as far as comfortable and then stand back up together. After a successful squat and stand have pairs high five and thank each other for being partners and keeping each other safe.**WARNING:** Each of these actions has its own safety issue – mostly footing issues. Identify and remove (if possible) any hazards and warn participants of any possible dangers. Again, these actions will put strain on certain muscle groups. Encourage participants to pay attention to their abilities. **Variations:** You could continue each action in groups of 4. You could also end with a group cheek-2-cheek which can be a good lead into another group challenge like Mono-Pod found in the Challenge and Problem Solving section.

Pass Your Own Name Game (learned at an impromptu comedy workshop) You'll need enough room to circle up your group. Works well with 8 to 25 players for 10 to 15 minutes. (If we have more than 16 players we make multiple circles.)

Process: This is an interesting name game that is much more challenging than it appears. Choose a player to start the action. The action is a player pointing to another player in the circle with an outstretched arm and hand and then saying his or her OWN name. The player pointed at chooses another player to point at and says his or her own name. Each player pointed at continues the action. If a mistake is made, after the laughing (with and not at), have the mistaken player restart with a point and a pass of his or her own name. The underlying challenge is to keep this activity going at a good pace – moving as quickly as possible. This adds to the excitement factor. We like to use this activity to point out that it is okay to make mistakes and when we laugh, we laugh with each other and not at each other – there is a difference. **Variations:** Sometimes we start out pointing and saying the name of the player we are pointing at – to learn names. Then we up the challenge by passing our own name. You could also change the objective into a Fun Filled Game. If a player makes a mistake they are asked to step out of the circle to observe (or be hecklers) the remainder of the game – playing down to the last few players standing.

"When you get it, then what?"

Hello (multiple sources) You'll need enough room to make a large circle with your group. Works well with 10 to 25 players for 10 to 14 minutes.

Process: This is an acquaintance variation of Eye Tag found in the Fun Filled Games section. Players form a circle and are asked to look down at the ground. The facilitator will say, "Look Up." At which time all the players look up and across the circle to one other player – no looking around to anyone else. If two players happen to make eye contact with each other they walk towards each other, across the circle, they shake hands exchange names and then move to the place in the circle left unoccupied by the person they just passed. Once all the movement is complete, the facilitator says, "Look Down" – every player looks down to the ground. Start the next round by saying, "Look Up" and the game goes on. Play as long as the energy is good. We like to challenge the participants to learn all the names of the players in the group – if they don't know each other yet. So, at the end of the activity you will be able to ask any player to tell you all the first names of every other player in the group. **Variations:** You can continue this game (or play it at another time) by stopping the action, then adding some information players must attain from each other. Like, finding out where everyone is from, how many brothers and sisters they have, or what is their favorite thing to do. So, the activity plays the same way: make eye contact with someone (most likely someone you need information from), cross to change places, shake hands, share names, find out the requested information, then move to the unoccupied spot. After stopping the activity, go around to each player and ask the rest of the group what they found out about him or her - nice way to break the ice.

Peter, Paul & Mary You'll need room enough to circle up your group. Works well with 8 to 16 per group – multiple groups can play – for 20 to 25 minutes.

Process: This game is played just like Ah-So-Ko found in FUNN Stuff, Vol. 1, by Karl Rohnke. You can have your group sitting or standing in a circle (Single Chicken Wing to the Left). Players use

three motions in order. The first is using either arm with the hand on the chest, fingers pointing to the left or right (depending on what arm is used of course). Second motion is an open hand on the head fingers pointing to the left or the right – depending on the arm used. The third motion is arm out, hand open, fingers pointing. The motions always follow this order - after the third motion, the player point-ed to per-forms

the first motion and so on. After making a motion the player doing so must say the name of the person the fingers are pointing to. That person then makes the next motion saying the name of the person he or she is pointing to.

This next player points to anyone in the circle, using the third motion, and says the persons name – the one she or he is pointing at. The game con-tinues with the first motion again. If a

28

mistake of any kind, incorrect motion or an incorrect name, is made by a player, he or she must find a new place in the circle and start the game again with the first motion. Fun factor: This game is meant to be played with gusto! Speed increases the opportunity to move to other places in the circle to learn more names (Okay, speed increases the mistake factor.) **Variations:** Karl's version includes the verbal sounds of, "Ahh, So, and Ko" with gusto. Same hand motions just replace the names with the sounds.

"If all in the past is done, what has the past done?"

My Baggage Lies Over The Ocean You'll need enough room to create one big circle with your group. Plays well with 10 to 25 (or more) for 12 to 17 minutes.

Process: This is a warm-up that includes the vocal cords – yes, this one's a singer. The song is sung to the tune of, "My Bonnie Lies over the Ocean." Just replace the words with the ones below. So, go ahead and practice.

> My Baggage Lies over the Ocean,
> My Baggage Lies over the Sea,
> My Baggage Lies over the Ocean,
> Oh, bring back my Baggage to me!
> Bring Back, Bring Back,
> Oh, Bring Back my Baggage to me to me.
> Bring Back, Bring Back,
> Oh, Bring Back my Baggage to me to me.

When the group has the words and the tune down, up the challenge. Singing the song again and have them clap on every "B" sound – mostly "Baggage" and several "Bring Backs." The group might want to try this a few times before practicing the next challenge. Perform a dip at the knees or stand back up on every other "B" sound – dipping on the first "Baggage" standing back up on the second "Baggage." Then dip at the next "Baggage" standing back up at the next and so on through the song. It works out to everyone standing back up on the last "Baggage." The triple challenge is to put the clapping and the dip/stand together. If the group is still having fun, give it another try a bit faster. **Variations:** If you dare, alternate Claps and Dips. Will they end up standing or dipped?

Making Connections You'll need enough space to end up in a large circle with your group. Plays well with 8 to 25 for 12 to 18 minutes.

Process: The ultimate objective for the group is to be linked up in a circle. One player is chosen to start (often times we as facilitators choose to start to role model the idea). This first player places her right hand on her hip making a link area with her elbow. She then begins to share true statements or qualities about herself to the group. (We like to encourage qualities that are not common knowledge or visually apparent like clothes or physical features. However, this might be okay for some groups). As soon as someone else in the group has something in common with one of her statements they move over to "link" arms with this person (this new player using his left to link with the first players right), then forming the next link with a right hand on the hip. The player that just linked up then starts making true statements or qualities about himself. This process keeps going until all are linked together. The last person must then be able to "link" back to the first player, through a true statement or quality, to close the circle – reaching the ultimate objective. **Variations:** You could use this process with the "Build a Story" game. The first player opens a story with, "Once upon a time in a well lit room." When someone in the group wants to add to that sentence they link up with the first player and continue the story, "Crowds of people gathered to hear the news." New players can then link on to build the story from there.

6-Count (shared by Sam Sikes) You'll need enough room for players to move their arms around freely. Plays well with 8 to 25 (or more) for 20 to 30 minutes.

Process: Make sure everyone has enough room to move their arms up and down straight out from their sides. Ask everyone to start with their arms down at their sides. First, everyone count to

6 – "One, Two, Three, Four, Five, Six." Good. Now using the left arm you're going to count and add some movement. On "One", a straight left arm goes up, out to the side and stops straight up overhead in the air. On "Two" back down to the side the same way. On "Three" the arm goes straight back up overhead. On "Four" is back down to the side. On "Five" straight up again, "Six" back down to the side. Good. Now some practice with the right arm. On "One" a straight right arm moves through the side stopping straight up overhead. On "Two" the right arm moves down but only half way, stopping when it is parallel to the ground. On "Three" the arm goes all the way back down to the side. At "Four" the arm goes all the way back up again, on "Five" down parallel to the ground, and on "Six" it's back down to the side. You might like to practice each arm one more time. The ultimate challenge is to put both arm movements together at the same time! (see the pictures provided for a double-arm visual.) Try this a few times starting out slow and building up speed. After some laughs stop the action. Let them know they can practice later on their own if they want to master it.

   If you think your group is ready for another challenge split them up into groups of 3 to 5 players. Have the small groups develop a system to perform the arm motions together as a group – synchronized 6- Count. After a few minutes of practicing, have each group, if they so choose to, perform their routine in front of the rest of the group. Remember, laughing with and not at. **Variations:** Before the group is split into smaller teams to work on the actions together we might choose to use this experience to emphasize a bit of our role as facilitators. There might be times when we will provide some information that might assist the group or participants. For example, on number "One" both hands are up on number "Six" both hands are down – this "guide" might move someone closer to their goal (they still have to do the work but there is some information). Also, if you separate out and teach them the "windmill" movement in the middle on "Three" and "Four" they can add to their base of knowledge to become even closer to success – almost 80% if they put the learning together. This little object lesson might come in handy down the road.

Double Jump 6-Count (variation of Six Count shared by a workshop participant) You'll need enough room for players to move their arms around freely. Plays well with 8 to 25 (or more) for 20 to 30 minutes.

Process: (Please review, Six Count above if you haven't tried that one yet.) In the Double Jump version, players again first count to 6 (just for practice). Then do the arm part of jumping jacks - counting to 6, "One" both arms up, "Two" both arms down, "Three" up, "Four" down, "Five" up, "Six" down – easy. Now, have the players practice the leg movements – a bit different than traditional Jumping Jacks. Starting with legs together players jump out, and stay out for "One" and "Two" (two bounces), back in for 1 jump on "Three", out for 2 bounces on "Four" and "Five" back in for the last bounce on "Six". So it's: out on "One" "and Two", in on "Three", out on "Four" and "Five", in on "Six". As you already expect, the ultimate challenge is to put both the arm and leg movements together. Double Jump 6-Count can be done on its own as an individual challenge. You can also progress into a team challenge - teaming up 4 or 5 players together and give them about 4 minutes to work out a "synchronized" double jump 6-count. The small groups will then be asked to voluntarily share their creations with the rest of the group – diverse performances can be expected through this teaming. **Variations:** Certain groups can have a great time making up their own 6-Count movements – a great creative activity process and more variations for you to share with others.

"Consider!"

34

Cooperation & Communication

Once the participants in your group know each other's names, have gotten a bit more comfortable around each other and have warmed up their muscles, you can move into the Cooperation & Communication activities. These activities demand a bit more verbal interaction and brain power. Facilitators will start to use their processing tools before, during, or after these activities to start focusing on the objectives the group came in with or are developing as their awareness unfolds. Many team and community building concepts will start to present themselves, such as Cooperation, Communication (which you already guessed), Participation, Leadership, Followership, Brainstorming, Sharing, Willingness, Effort, Support and more. The facilitator's role is to guide the group toward their own learning - allowing them to answer their own questions and let them discover what they already know.

Are You More Like You'll need a mid-size open area. Plays well with 8 to 25 (or more) for 15 to 20 minutes.
Process: You might want to prepare your own list of, "Are you more like…?" questions before hand if the examples below don't fit for you. (The examples are taken from the book *"Are you more like…? 1001 Colorful Quandaries for Quality Conversations"* by Chris Cavert and Susana Acosta-Cavert. (See the Resource section for more info). Gather the group in front of you, facing in your direction, and ask them an, "Are you more like…?" question. Indicate that if they are more like the first thing you said, move over to their left, if they are more like the second thing you said move over to the right – creating an apparent gap between the two choices. (If you want to play with "undecided," players can stay in the gap. As for us, we ask them to make a choice.) Before giving another question, ask the players to look around to see who else

35

made the same choice you did – looking for commonalities. Continue the process as long as the energy is good. **Variations:** After a few questions we might turn it over to the group to ask an, "Are you more like..?" question. With smaller groups you might take the time to ask some players why they made the choice they did. In our experience most of the younger groups tend to choose their favorite of the two. Older groups can be encouraged to make the "metaphorical" jump into how they are "like" or similar to their choice – complex thinking skills.

Examples: Are you more like....

the accelerator or the brakes?
action or suspense?
an autobiography or a biography?
a basket or shopping cart?

a boomerang or a Frisbee®?
a bus or a plane?
caffeinated or decaffeinated?
cash or charge?
city lights or stars?

Coke-a-cola® or Pepsi®?
a comic book or a history book?
cookies or rice cakes?
crayons or paint?
a cruise or a hike?
cupid or the tooth fairy?
a crumpler or a folder?
a song or a dance?
a deli or a diner?
the desert or the jungle?
dinner or lunch?
a drawing or a painting?

dynamic rope or static rope?
an e-mail or a phone call?
an escalator or the stairs?
exercise bike or a treadmill?
an explorer or a settler?
an extrovert or an introvert?

a ferris wheel or a merry-go-round?
a follower or a leader?
a foot or a hand?
the foundation or the structure?
a frame or a picture?
full service or self service?
the lawn or the garden?
a glance or a look?
going or staying?
a gulper or a sipper?
hamburgers or hotdogs?
a hand written or typed letter?
the tortoise or the hare?
head lights or tail lights?
a hiking trail or a sidewalk?
the hook or the line?
a hot tub or a sauna?
ice skates or roller blades?
indoors or outdoors?
infinite or limited?
insatiable or satisfied?
international or national?
a jester or a king (or Queen)?
the key or the lock?
a lake or a pool?
a small group or a large group?

a letter or a postcard?
a listener or a talker?
loud or quiet?
a Mac or a PC?
a main course or a side dish?
mild or spicy?
a morning person or night person?
a movie or a play?
nine iron or a putter?
noon or midnight?
an only child or a sibling?
an opera or a rodeo?
an optimist or a pessimist?
pants or shorts?
park or a playground?
a paper clip or a rubber band?
a peak or a valley?
salt or pepper?
pig out or work out?
plain or peanut?
work or play?
a player or spectator?
please or thank you?
a poem or a story?
the post or the sign?
potato chips or pretzels?
a principal or a teacher?
private school or public school?
radio or television?
a rainbow or a thunderstorm?
a reaction or a response?
"Read between the lines" or "Say it like it is"?
a reader or a writer?

recycle it or toss it?
the rose or the thorns?
sandals or shoes?
Saturday or Sunday?
a saver or a spender?
school or vacation?
scientific or theological?
self service or a waiter?
the shade or the sun?
shoes or socks?
a shout or a whisper?
a sled or skis?
a slide or a swing?
smart or stupid?
snow skiing or water skiing?
a spaceship or a submarine?
Spiderman® or Superman®?
spots or stripes?
a stapler or a staple?
stop or yield?
a student or a teacher?
the sunrise or the sunset?
a taco or a tamale?
a test or a quiz?
this or that?
a three ring binder or spiral notebook?
to be or not to be?
a trick or a treat?
Tupperware® or Ziplocks®?
typing or handwriting?
Velcro® or zippers?
a weekday or weekend?

Back-to-Back (shared by Jim Cain) You'll need a good size area to move around in. Plays well with 12 to 25 (or more) for 15 to 25 minutes.

Process: This is a simple technique used to get acquainted with others more personally. Back-to-Back also works very well to quiet a group down – most people standing back-to-back don't talk to each other (it's a great technique to use when you need the groups attention). Ask everyone to stand back-to-back with one other player (even numbers work best for this). You'll notice

the noise level of the group go down. While the players are standing back-to-back give the group a discussion question (open-ending question) like, "Discuss the type of car you drive (or would like to be driving)" or "Describe the perfect meal." Then you will say, "Face-to-face!" At this point everyone walks to a NEW partner to discuss the question – they do not discuss the question with the person they were back-to-back with. (Make sure to provide a designated space for players to find each other if needed

– the center of the room works best.) With their new partner they discuss the question given until they hear, "Back-to-back!" again. At this time, players turn back-to-back with the person they were just talking to and wait for the next discussion question or instructions. **Variations:** Other possible questions might be: What would you do with a million dollars? Where would you like to go on your next vacation? Describe your dream house. What would you ask the President if you had 5 minutes of his time? What would you like to be doing 5 years from now? If you had a day off (from school or work) what would you do? If you could change one thing about school/work, what would it be? Describe the scariest thing that ever happened to you? What was the last thing you did to help another person? What would you like to learn how to do and why? If you could have lunch with anyone who would it be and what would you talk about?

Building a Handshake (learned from Frank Fry) You need a nice size open space to move around in. Plays well with 10 to 24 players (even numbers work best for this one – so you might get to play!!) for 15 to 25 minutes.

Process: Pair up players and have them create a sequenced greeting handshake of some sort – one with 2 to 3 different "moves" included. For example, a high five followed by an index finger link shake followed by a fist-to-fist touch. Give each pair a few minutes to master their greeting. When everyone has had enough time to practice ask the players to find a new partner. Players then share their last greeting with this new partner. The challenge is then to combine the two greetings together using all the movements of both greetings – they don't necessarily have to be in the same order (but most keep them that way). Give the pairs ample

41

time to memorize this new combination greeting. If you dare, ask the players to find a new partner again – someone they have not done a greeting with. Can this new pair combine their newest greeting into one mega-handshake? If time allows you could have pairs share their handshake with the rest of the group. **Variations:** Have pairs come up with a sentence that rhymes, like, "Once you find your way there you can stay." Each pair commits their rhyme to memory. Create new pairs that put their rhymes together. Remember this combination and find another partner to add to the poem. Pairs can rearrange lines to make it work. If they can, pair up a fourth time for another line (hey that rhymes!)

3-D Categories (shared by Neil Mercer) You'll need a nice open area for your participants to move around in. Plays well with 16 to 25 (or more) for 20 to 30 minutes.

Process: This one is based upon the good old Categories activity. A group of any size is asked to clump together according to a like subject, for example, least favorite food, most exotic place traveled to, most favorite food, number of brothers and sisters, number of pets at the moment and so on.

In 3-D Categories the group members, having the same preference, create a static or dynamic statue or animation of their preference so the rest of the group can guess what the preference is. Some interesting 3-Ds might include zodiac sign, favorite mode of transportation, favorite season, favorite type of pet, favorite animal found in the forest or sea, favorite subject in school, favorite ride at the amusement park, most frequented fast food restaurant in your life. **Variations:** You could also use this same 3-D process with an activity called Commonalities. Ask the participants to get into small groups of 4 or 5 and find something, through talking and sharing, that they have in common with each other. The challenge is then to create a 3-D formation, static or dynamic, statue or animation, that will be shared with the rest of the group who then tries to figure out what the presenters all have in common.

See Ya (variation of the activity, Get Lost from *No Supplies* Required) You'll need a good size open area. Plays well with 20 to 25 (or more) for 20 to 25 minutes.

Process: Ask your group to split up into groups of 4 to 5 players. Have each group stand apart from each other so they have their own personal group space. Have everyone in the small groups introduce themselves to each other (if they don't know each other yet). First, you'll need to teach everyone a couple of skills. Inform the groups that the number of players in their group at this time will always be the number of players in that group (not necessarily the same players). Now, on to the skills. Skill one: No player may leave the group until they hear the words, "See Ya!" The group will say, "See Ya" after the facilitator says, "Ready?" (more on this in a minute). Skill two: When someone leaves a group the remaining players wave their arms and hands up in the air stating, "OVER HERE, OVER HERE! OVER…." (hopefully with a little gusto) until a NEW player joins their group – remember always the same number of players in the group. You might want to practice the, "OVER HERE'S" for a few seconds – with feeling.

   With these skills down the game can begin. Give all the groups a discussion question, like, "Tell each other the last movie you saw and if you liked it or not." Give them all about 60 seconds to share – giving a 15 second warning before the time is up. When time is up, ask the group a "determining" question, like, "Determine who has the shortest hair in your circle." Give about 15 seconds. Explain that when you say, "Ready" the rest of the group will say, "See Ya!" and the pre-determined player must leave their group and join another group (players yelling, "OVER HERE, OVER HERE!"). Once everyone has joined a new group have players introduce each other, then, give them another discussion question, like, "If you could go on a $1000 shopping spree, where would you go and what would you buy?" After 90 seconds ask a determining question, like, "Who is the person with the darkest eyes?" and then send them off to a new group after, "See Ya." Five or six rounds usually holds the interest. **Variations:** Here are some other Determiners for you: Tallest person, shortest person, shoe size – largest or smallest, most jewelry, the whitest socks (or ankles), the oldest parents or grandparents, the most cousins, the most pets in their lifetime, has owned the largest pet (is a horse a pet or a mode of transportation? Do you ride any other sort of pet?), longest hair, dirtiest fingernail area, longest fingernails or the last person to stick their tongue out.

   Body Language   (shared by Karl Rohnke) This one can be done with limited space or an open area. Plays well with 10 to 25 for 15 to 25 minutes.

   Process: Have small groups of 4 to 5 players work together to come up with a word they will be able to spell out using their bodies to form the letters. We like to do this in "presentation

style." Have groups huddle together to come up with a word and then do some "stealthy" practice – might want to come up with a backup word just in case. When all the groups are ready have each, in turn, present their word for the other groups to decipher. If you have enough players, split into larger small groups to form longer words. End up with all the players together making one word (or two) for the photographic moment. **Variations:** Use this as a Fun Filled Game by keeping score. The first group to say the word presented receives a point. When presenting, ask the group to line up in their "ready" position and then "snap" their letters/word into place. You could also play a type of "un-scramble." Groups present a word with the letters out of order and the other groups have to un-scramble the letters to find the word for a score.

Line up in a Circle (from Neil Mercer) You'll need a mid-size open area. Plays well with 12 to 25 for 10 to 15 minutes.

Process: Have your group get into a Chicken Dumplings formation (see The Chicken Game in Frontloaders). While standing still (players cannot adjust their position) the participants are instructed to look around there area and identify the person who is standing closest to them on the right hand side of their body and the person who is standing closest to them on the left hand side of their body – talking is allowed. When the group is ready say, "Go!" At this point the group, the members of the group, as quickly as possible, are to arrange themselves in such a way that each participant is standing directly next to those two people they determined were to their right and left. If someone in the group has a chronometer (fancy word for a stop-watch) on their wrist, you could time the process. After a circle is made have the group mingle around meeting and greeting others. Call, "Chicken Dumplings" so each player is again within their own personal space. When the group lets you know they are ready, give them a, "GO!" Does the process improve over several rounds by a time standard? **Variations:** You could give everyone a number (a bit more memory involved here) so after the Chicken Dumplings players circle up by number. For an ultra-challenge, during the mingle have players exchange numbers during their handshakes – left/right brain activity.

Switch, Change & Rotate (learned from Mike Spiller) You'll need a nice big open area for this one. Works well with 20 or more for 20 to 25 minutes.

Process: Ask your players to get into groups of 3 or 4 and stand in a single-file line facing in the same direction. This activity involves the facilitator giving specific commands the small groups are asked to follow - to the best of their ability. First you'll want to do some practicing with the small groups standing in place. The first command is, "Switch." The player at the front of the line peels off and goes to the back of the line – practice. Next, say "Change." The line of players is required to turn 180 degrees to face the opposite direction – practice. Next is "Rotate." This command requires the front and back players to exchange places – practice. Spend a little time practicing with each command while the groups are stationary. At this point you are going to add the command, "Move." On this command the groups start walking (doesn't need to be fast) around the room (within the established boundary area) in their single file line formation – the head of the line being the leader. The lines are allowed to weave around the area as long as each small group stays together. The last command you will need to give the groups is, "Freeze" – this obviously stops all the action. So, now the groups have all the commands they need. Here is the ultimate challenge. Start out the groups with, "Move" then begin working in the Switch, Change & Rotates as the groups are walking around. (If you have some music to play during the activity it gives the groups some beat to walk to.) Give the groups enough time between calls to get into the correct formation. Be sure to mix up the "commands" so the groups do not know in what order the commands will be given!! After a few minutes the groups should have it down pretty well. This activity brings you wonderful leadership issues and how the group members help one another. **Variations:** If you think your group is ready for a trusting challenge, have them first, "Freeze" in place. Ask them to close their eyes for the next round. Assure the players they can open their eyes at any time if they need to but challenge them to work together to keep this safe. Also, teach the "Bumpers Up" position (hands and arms up in front of you with thumbs touching) to add some up-front safety.

The Folds (discovered in a 1950s game book) No special space needs. Plays well with 2 to 25 (or more) for 10 to 15 minutes.

Process: Ask the players to imagine this puzzle in their head – they my not use any props to solve this. "Imagine you have an 8 ½ by 11 sheet of paper in your head. Fold this paper in half. Now, fold the paper in half again, but make this second fold perpendicular to the first fold. The puzzle is, if you were to cut this folded paper, making the cut parallel to the first fold, how many separate pieces of paper would you get?" From this point ask the players in the group to get together with people who have the same answer as they do. If there is more than one group, have players try and convince a player in another group to agree with the answer that they have. The objective would be to reach consensus on one number before the answer is revealed. This is an activity we use to work on consensus building. How will players convince or demonstrate enough information to get others to agree with them? What is the answer? Hmmmm…what sort of a facilitators would we be if we told you? What is your answer?

Human Knot-So-Fast (the earliest reference I found for this one is in *The New Games Book*) You'll need enough room for your group(s) to end up standing in a circle. Plays well with 8 to 25 for 17 to 24 minutes.

Process: This activity has been a staple for many adventure programs down through the years. Some like it for its unknown outcome – in a random setup there are several possible answers. We like to set this one up so that we know it will end up in a circle formation. Ask your group to form circles of 8 – 12 players and hold hands (this will be referred to as the First Circle). At this point have the players commit to memory the player to their right and the player to their left – names, eye color, clothes, whatever helps. When that is done ask everyone to rearrange their circles so that each player is standing next to two new players within the same circle (this will be referred to as the Second Circle). Now, to set up the knot, have each player find the two players from the First Circle (the ones they committed to memory). Players then reconnect hands (across this Second Circle they created) with those First Circle players –

holding the same hands they did in that First Circle. The challenge is then to untangle the arms, without breaking hand-to-hand contact, into what will eventually be the First Circle formation. If a group gets "stuck" you might allow them one "break" and re-grasp, however, everyone will need to agree where the one break will occur – good consensus building. **Variation:** The traditional versions starts with groups of 8 to 12 players in a circle. From here everyone reaches into the center of the circle with their right hand and grabs hold of the right hand of someone "across" the circle from them – not a player standing next to them. Next, players take their left hand and grab the left hand of someone else across the circle, making sure they do not grab the same person's hand they are already holding. Without turning lose of hands, the group is challenged to "untie" the Human Knot they created. This random setup has multiple solutions – one full circle, two or more circles "linked" together, or multiple circles un-linked.

"Always better than one."

Trust & Support Building

This section is filled with activities that will enhance and focus on developing Trust and Support within the group. The activities in the previous sections helped to establish a foundation of togetherness and sharing. At some level Trust and Support are being built through common goals and achievement. The activities that follow will demand more of an awareness of physical safety needs and the emotional needs of self and others. Some might consider these activities to be more "risky" in relation to others - involving more physical and emotional risk. The facilitator's number one responsibility to the group is to keep it safe. Physical safety needs are usually more apparent where emotional needs are less visible. Over time the facilitator should be able to recognize the emotional needs of a group as easily as the physical needs. Always keep in mind, it is easier to build trust one small step at a time than it is to build trust back up after it is lost - don't do too much too soon. Be safe and be well!

Trio Trust Lean (traditional trust/spotting activity) You'll want plenty of open space for small groups to work safely. Plays well with 3 to 25 for 20 to 30 minutes.

Process: Divide your group into smaller groups of 3 or 4 players. One person will assume the "trusting" or active position – this involves crossing the arms over the chest with the body nice and straight – solid as a board. The two other participants will be the "spotters" in a "spotter's position" behind the active player (see first photo). The spotting position (as seen in the picture) is knees bent, legs ready to be strong but giving, arms up and bent ready to be strong but giving and the hands open with fingers together. Spotters are to maintain physical contact with the active participant during the beginning of the activity – hands will be on the active

player's shoulder blades. When everyone is in position the active player must use a set of commands before leaning back. The active player asks, "Spotters Ready?" The spotters, in their spotting stance with their hands on the active player's shoulder blades answer, "Ready!" (if there is any question about their readiness, the active participant may ask again). Then the active participant states, "Ready to trust!" (this means, ready to lean back). The response from the spotters is, "Trust us _____" (using the name of the participant). At this point the active participant leans (or some might say "falls" back – we seem to stay away from the word FALL for some reason) back towards the spotters. The spotters, bending in their arms a bit, let the active participant lean back to experience a trusting moment. The spotters then, carefully set the active player back up to standing. (If there is a fourth player in the group, he can be standing in front of the active player as a spotter preventing this person from tipping forward too far.) If the active participant is willing to do another lean, the spotters back up a little bit – they don't need to touch the leaner initially this time.

The group follows the same process as above, this time with a bit more trust involved – more lean. If willing, spotters can go another step back so the active player can go for a "mean" lean. Make sure everyone in the small groups has the chance to practice at each position – both spotting positions and the leaner. **Note:** The facilitator(s) should be walking around among the groups giving corrective and encouraging feedback. **WARNING:** This activity must be conducted with all seriousness. "Safety Joking" is not appropriate – ever! **Variations:** For a bit more excitement ask the active participant (the leaner) to close his or her eyes during the lean.

Tick-Tock (earliest reference we found is from Karl Rohnke) You'll want plenty of open space for small groups to work safely. Works well with 3 to 25 players for 20 to 30 minutes.

Process: Tick-Tock is a nice variation to the Trio Trust Lean – a bit more trusting in this one (we suggest you review the Trio Lean above if you haven't done so yet). Divide your group into smaller groups of 3 players (you can form group of four if needed, participants will just have to take turns at each position). As in the Trio Lean above, there will be one "trusting" or active participant and two spotters. The difference is that one spotter will be behind the active participant and one will be in front (see picture). Again, the first set up is done where the spotters stand close enough to touch the active participant – the front spotter places her hands on the crossed arms of the active participant. When everyone is ready the active participant goes through the commands (described in Trio Trust Lean) and then leans back. At this point the back spotter CAREFULLY pushes (not hard) the active participant back up and past standing into the hands of the front spotter who then lets the active participant do some forward leaning. The action continues with the front spotter pushing (again, CAREFULLY) the active participant back over into the hands of the back spotter. This Tick-Tock motion is done a few times to give the active participant a bit of an experience. It's also important to note that the active participant will have a much better experience if he or she keeps her or his body "straight as a board" and avoid just bending at the hips. If the active participant is willing the spotters can move back for a deeper Tick-Tock motion. SAFETY, SAFETY, SAFETY! Participants switch out positions so each has a chance in all three areas.

Leadership Mirroring (variation of the traditional follow-the-leader activity) You'll need enough room for pairs to work together comfortably. Works well with 2 to 24 (or more) for 15 to 25 minutes.

Process: This activity popped back up at an impromptu stand-up comedy workshop. The leadership lesson in it was impressive. Pair up players in your group and have the players in each pair face each other. Ask the player who lives furthest from the point they are standing go first. This player is designated the "leader" of the pair for the first round. She will be making movements that her partner will be following. The leader must always be in front of her partner and there should be no physical contact made during the action. So, the leader can move around her arms, hands, head, face, body in any form or fashion they so desire and the other person must (at the same time) "mirror" what the leader is doing. Leaders are free to move laterally as well keeping in mind the stipulations. This is not a "catch-the-player-doing-something-wrong" activity. It's more of a "dance" between the two players. (The reason this activity is in the Trust & Support Building section is because of the embarrassment risk – people tend to be very self-conscious about looking silly.) After a minute or so have the partners switch roles – the first leader is now the follower. For the third round ask that neither of the partners be the leader (this was the impressive part). What happens? The interesting thing is that leadership does take place, however, it tends to shift back and forth from one partner to the other. Take a little time to discuss with the group what happened during the third round – a nice leadership object lesson.

Variations: To make this even more of a leadership experience you could have pairs give feedback (a constructive social skill) to each other about the way the leader lead the "dance."

Leadership Walk (variation of a Karl Rohnke activity) You'll need an interesting area to take an adventure walk through – wooded path, nature trail, hallways with stairs, combination of indoor and outdoor walk, etc. Plays well with 10 to 25 players for 30 to 40 minutes.

Process: First you might need to split your group into two smaller groups. If you have 16 or more players go ahead and make two groups. Also, if you create two groups you will need a facilitator with each group (we advise you not to do this activity if you do not have another facilitator to observe the second group). When the group is (or groups are) ready have them choose, by consensus and

55

agreement (also by the ones chosen) 2 players to be the leaders of the first leg of the Leadership Walk. When the leaders are chosen they step out of the group. The part of the group being lead will get in a single-file line, place their right hands in the shoulders of the players in front of them and then close their eyes. One of the challenges for the group members will be to keep their eyes closed until the "destination" is met (however, if they need to open their eyes they do have that choice). When the group is ready the leaders then use their "communication" skills (talking and touching are allowed – you can tell them this or not) to lead the group on the Walk. The facilitator with the group will visually show the leaders what path they want them to take – this will depend on "where" the group is at in their development together. Keep in mind, the more interesting the walk the better the experience. However, you also want to keep it safe so the trust level is going up not down. åRemember, the facilitator (that's you) is ultimately responsible for the group! Back to the walk. After a few minutes, stop the group and ask the players being lead to open their eyes. At this point we like to open a feedback session about how the leaders did during the walk. (You might need to do some skill building around feedback before this activity if needed.) The idea is to provide information about leadership – what is needed and what is helpful. The ultimate goal (as you know) is to use this information in the future – which is coming right up. When the discussion is concluded the group chooses two more leaders for the next leg of the walk. And so the process repeats. Allow an opportunity for each player to be a leader – one player might need to go a second time with a partner if there is an odd number of players in the group. **Variations:** We have also done this activity with all the players closing their eyes, right hand on shoulders. The leadership here is the player in front. The facilitator uses physical contact with the first leader to direct the path. After a minute or so, rotate the last player in line up to the front (this rotation seems to be the most interesting because the back player always seems to know what the leader should be doing!?).

Human Maze You'll need a nice open space for this one. Plays well with 16 to 25 for 30 to 40 minutes.

Process: Pair up your players (if you need to make a group of 3 make sure this group is the first to negotiate the maze – in this way they will be the first and the last group to negotiate). Initially, designate half the group (half the pairs) to be the maze and the other half to be the negotiators of the maze. Each maze pair will create a certain obstacle negotiators have to get through (notice the picture) - forming tunnels, turns, step-overs, etc. Maze pairs should be far enough apart from each other so as not to create a "clog" in the maze. The negotia-tor pairs include one player with his eyes closed and the other player (eyes open) being the guide – who guides the blinded player through the maze obstacles. The sighted guide is only allowed to give verbal directions to her unsighted partner. When the maze is ready to go the first pair of negotiators begins the maze. After they are through

the first obstacle the second pair begins the maze as the first pair proceeds to the next obstacle and so on. When the first pair negotiates all the obstacles in the maze the unsighted player can open his eyes. This pair then becomes an obstacle in the maze for the following negotiators. Back at the beginning of the maze, when the last pair of negotiators from the first group of negotiators completes the first obstacle, made by a pair from the first group of

57

"mazers," this pair of mazers (who were the first obstacle) become negotiators – they start to negotiate the maze with one unsighted player and a guide (you may want to go back and diagram that if it would help!?). So, the idea is sort of a leap-frog method of action.

 If you have the room the maze may turn out to proceed in a line of obstacles or if you are in a closed area the maze would take on a circle form. To review, after negotiating the maze, and there are no more obstacles ahead of you, you become a part of the maze. When there are no more players waiting to negotiate your obstacle your pair becomes negotiators. This cycle happens twice so both players get the chance to go through the maze unsighted. **Note:** As the facilitator you might need to help the group keep track of where the maze begins (if the maze forms a circle) so players know when to transition – the line maze is self-evident. **Variations:** Of course the traditional Partner Walk is where a sighted player leads her unsighted partner through a natural obstacle walk like through a wooded path or configuration of furniture in a room or physical education equipment in a gym.

Eagle Trust Run (learned from Sam Sikes) You'll need a very large open area to work in, especially if you have to create more than one group. Plays well with 7 to 25 for 25 to 35 min.

Process: This is a very powerful activity when it is kept safe – so, please keep it safe. If you need to make two (or more) groups there must be a facilitator with each group. We split our group when we have 14 or more players – we don't play this one with less than 7 in a group. Here's the overall look. Each group will have one active participant for each round. The remainder of the group creates a large circle (a little bit beyond the Flying Chicken circle described in The Chicken Game - I guess we could call this one the Circle Formation Solo Flying Chicken). This circle of players will be spotters (or in this case we could call them – guiders). The active participant will start by standing in the middle of her groups circle with her eyes closed and her arms up – like the Flying Chicken. From here she will start to slowly (emphasize slowly) jog towards the circle of players. As the active participant (the Eagle) approaches the spotters the one nearest the Eagles right arm carefully takes this arm with both hands, holding above the Eagles wrist, and turns her around the outside of the circle and then brings her back to the inside of the circle and gently lets go so the Eagle is traveling across the inside of the circle again towards another spotter. (As you can envision, you don't want a "crack-the-whip" sort of turn and let go – this would not build trust. It is a gentle turn back into the circle.) The Eagle continues across the circle where another spotter,

closest to the Eagles right arm, turns the Eagle back into the circle again. Let the Eagle take 3 or 4 crosses before stopping the flight. Have the Eagle then exchange places with someone else in the circle ready to fly. **WARNING:** As with all trust activities, there are safety issues. Players need to pay attention, especially about knowing which arm (the right) of the Eagle to grab hold of. It will not build trust if two players each grab an arm of the Eagle at the same time. Also, spotters (or guiders) should not "whip" the Eagle around. This action can cause major spills. If you have any apprehension about your group performing this one safely, then do something else until you feel they can.

NETSIL (a classic blind line-up activity) You'll need an area large enough for your group to line up in. Works best with 12 to 25 players for 15 to 20 minutes.
Process: Ask the group to get into a Chicken Dumplings formation (see The Chicken Game in Frontloaders) and then close their eyes. Explain to the group they are to remain where they are with their eyes closed until you take them by the shoulders and gently lead them to a new location. As you move each player whisper a number in their ear that they are not to share verbally with anyone else in the group. Once all the participants have been placed (not close, but not to far away from each other), then explain that they must keep their eyes closed until you indicate it's time to open them and they can not share their assigned number using the "spoken" word. The challenge for them is to line up numerically and then "prove" to you that they have indeed accomplished the task before they can open their eyes or talk again. So, in short, you will be assigning a number (1 to however many) to each player while they have their eyes closed. When each player has a number they can begin to get themselves in number order without using any sort of language. Then, in some way, they must prove they are in order before the facilitator gives them instructions to open their eyes.
WARNING: Since players have their eyes closed make sure they are using the "bumpers up" hand position you taught them and watch for strays as they play – always keeping things safe. We like to use a "FREEZE" command for emergencies that requires all players to stop. When the safety issue is corrected the game can continue.

Variations: Another classic blind line-up activity is giving every player the name of an animal (one that makes a sound is best) and have the group line up smallest to largest animal by noise – more than one player can have the same animal noise.

Starting Line (adapted from a Bethel College Professor by Sean McFeely) You'll need a nice long open area – a place where a "race" can be run safely. Works well with 10 to 25 (or more) for 20 to 25 minutes.

Process: This activity deals with race, class, family and other related issues. Mr. McFeely uses this activity to help people appreciate and become more aware of the assets they have been raised with and the things in their upbringing which can be a challenge. Tell the group they are going to have a race. The objective is to be the first to cross the finish line (Sean sometimes uses a candy bar, "the first to get the candy bar" as an incentive for finishing first). Initially the group is asked to stand side-by-side toeing an established line you set (there will be an assumption that this is the starting line, however...). But, before you start the race each player in the group must answer some questions for themselves. Players will be asked to step forward or backward depending on their answer. Use the questions below (at least 6 or 7 from each list), alternating between stepping forward and stepping back.

WARNING: After reading the questions you might guess the possible issues this activity will bring up. Be mindful of what group you use this with – the right activity for the right group. Allow enough time for an open discussion afterwards.

When you have completed your list of questions, have the players look around to observe each others new "starting" positions. At this point you can say, "Ready? GO!" Invariably (in Sean's experience) the person with the most positive assets in their life (the one that stepped forward the most) scores the candy bar. The folks in the back [most likely] don't even try running the race. (Great metaphor to work with!) This activity really brings home the concept that the starting line (what is the "starting line" for people) might not seem as fair for everyone. Some obvious debrief avenues are, What might the candy bar represent in society?; Do you agree or disagree with the questions and the directions you were asked to go?; What other things are assets and detriments?, etc."

Variations: You might have candy bars available for everyone (around snack time) and as you pass them out you could ask each player what the "candy bar" is for him or her.

Take One Step Forward Questions

If you have a trust fund, own stock or have/will inherit money
Both parents are still married
Completed High School, Parents completed High School
In College, Parents completed College
Graduate Degree, Parents have degree
Scholarship or Parents Paid for Education
If one parent stayed at home while growing up
Parents owned your home
If you have a car
If your parents gave you a car
You had or have a significant mentor in your life
Had a job while in High School
Went to church growing up
If you were written up in the newspaper for something positive
If you were part of a youth group or community organizations (scouts, boys/girls club, 4H)
If a family or friend connection has ever gotten you a job
If you get together with extended family more than 4x a year.
If you have ever done volunteer work

Take One step back

If you moved more than 5 times growing up

For each person who gave you verbal or physical abuse

For each parent that works more than one job

If your family ever received any form of government assistance

If both parents were unemployed for more than a year

If you are not white

For each family member who was ever in jail or arrested

If you were part of a gang

If you were written up in the paper for something negative

One parent was not part of your life growing up for more than five years.

If raised in foster care or adopted

If your parents were never married

If you have seen anyone arrested.

If you were ever arrested

Pregnant as a teen or fathered a child

Suspended or expelled from school

10k of school or credit card debt

For each person in your home who had a drug or alcohol addiction

Running in the Dark (learned from Karl Rohnke way back when) You'll need a nice big open space to run in. Plays well with 7 to 25 for 20 to 30 minutes.

Process: This is a blind running activity. So, safety is, again, of the utmost importance. If you have more than 14 players in your group you can make two groups. We like to provide at least 60 feet of running room – and some extra for the over-run area. The runner will stand about 60 feet from the remainder of the group who is forming an open "V" shaped gauntlet – the wide part of the "V" is open towards the runner and the small end of the "V" is open at least 6 feet. Before beginning the runner will initiate some calls. First the runner asks, "Spotters Ready?" at which time the spotters in the gauntlet need to have their hands up and be mindful of the runner. The spotters then reply, "Ready!" The runner says, "Running!" The spotters respond, "Run Away!" At this point the runner closes her eyes and starts to run, as fast as possible, towards the gauntlet of spotters. The spotters responsibility at this point is to first move the gauntlet, if needed, from side to side in relation to where the runner is going – the spotters want the runner to end up going into the gauntlet. The second responsibility of the spotters (and most important) is to make contact with the runner to indicate to her that it is time to slow down and stop (see picture). It is very important that the spotters use their hands to "touch" the runner (like going through the brushes of a car wash) and not "grab" the runner. The touch will indicate to the runner it is time to stop, a grab can cause a sudden stop (or clothes-line as some know it) that might cause an injury. The gauntlet is there to protect and indicate the end of the run, not stop the runner from running. After the run have the runner become a part of the gauntlet so another player can take a turn. Provide enough time for each player to run twice – the first time there is usually some hesitation (less trust in the process), the second time there is usually more commitment (more trust) to the run. **Note:** If you create two groups it is best to have a facilitator with each group, however, with one facilitator you can manage the start of each group so they do not run at the same time.

Cookie Machine (variation of an activity from the New Games people) You'll need a mid-size open area for this one. Plays well with 20 to 25 (or more) for 25 to 35 minutes.

Process: Divide your group in half and have the two groups face each other about three feet apart. Keeping in mind proper "spotting and safety" techniques, have the group form a "zipper" by positioning their arms waist high, hands opened, palms up (notice in the picture). Slowly walking forward, have the players slide their arms down the side of the arms of the person across from them until their finger tips line up with that person's elbows - maintaining the waist high, hands open, palms up position. Make sure players on both sides of the "cookie machine" remain shoulder to shoulder with the persons next to them. Now for the fun. Have a volunteer, standing on

65

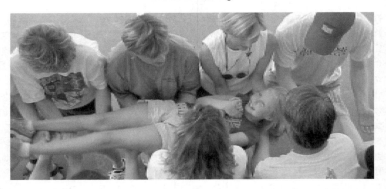

one end of the cookie machine, announce her favorite "cookie" to the group. Assuming the "trusting" position with her back to the cookie machine conveyer belt, similar to the Trio Trust Lean position above, the volunteer leans back onto the cookie machine conveyor belt – you will want to have the first few players at the end of the cookie machine safely help the volunteer onto the belt. Once the person is fully supported from head to feet, have the cookie machine gently toss, and at the same time pass, the raw cookie dough down the conveyor belt shouting out what type of cookie she is as they move her along. At the other end of the cookie machine a freshly baked cookie appears. Once the volunteers head reaches the end of the conveyer belt her shoulders are supported while her feet are set down to the ground. The players supporting her shoulders set her up to standing. Keep'm safe!! After the cheers, set up the lines again for another cookie pass. **WARNING:** Be present at the end of the line to supervise how the player is being set down. The participants supporting the shoulders are the last to let go. **Variations:** In the original New Games variation the volunteer is passed overhead – still a viable alternative if the group is ready. We would do this after the Levitation activity if we have a large group – enough players to form a nice long conveyer belt.

Touching the Sky (learned from Karl Rohnke) You don't need a lot of room for this one – being outside is the best place. Plays well with 11 to 13 people per group (multiple groups can play at the same time) for 25 to 35 minutes.

Process: You'll need no less than 11 players in a group. If you make two groups you must have a facilitator with each group. First you need to divide the group (or groups) in half and have each half form a line, each line facing each other (we're setting up just like the zipper in Cookie Machine above). Next, ask for a player (the active participant) who would like to be lifted assume the trusting position (as in Trio Trust Lean above) in the middle of the two lines. At this point the lines of players (the spotters) get ready to lift the active participant standing in the middle of the lines. The active participant initiates proper commands, "Spotters Ready?" Spotters, some ready to support the shoulders and upper body, others ready to lift the legs, respond, "Ready!" The active participant states, "Ready to Trust!" The spotters respond, "Trust us _____" (player's name). At this point the active participant leans back into the arms of the spotters. Have the two spotters nearest the active participant's head support the head with their nearest hand. The spotters closest to the legs pick up the lower torso and legs and reform their part of

67

the zippered lines – as in Cookie Machine above. The active participant is now lying in a bed of arms. At this point the spotters slowly
raise the participant up to the sky to the limit of the shortest spotter's
reach. The spotters can then hold the participant there for a few
moments. (The experience is extra powerful if the active participant
can keep his eyes open!) When ready, the spotters slowly lower
the player down. We like to use what Tom Smith calls, "grounding
the participant back to the earth." The spotters, keeping their backs
nice and straight, carefully lower the participant all the way to the
ground. Once the participant is down the spotters pull their hands
from under, and place them on top of the participant pressing down
lightly "grounding" the person to safety (This part is very powerful
for the active participant if he has his eyes closed!) Once the player
is grounded the spotters can help him up to standing. **Note:** As
you might have already considered, this is a very serious type of
activity. It can be a very powerful bonding experience for the group.
With this in mind, facilitate the energy where it needs to be.

Variations: Some facilitators like to add a rocking motion,
movement from head-to-toe, during the lifting and lowering part of
the activity – stopping the rocking for a still look at the sky.

Eskimo Toss (traditional activity without the blanket)
You need a mid-size open area with some good overhead room.
Plays well with 12 to 25 for 25 to 35 minutes.

Process: (If we have 24 players we'll create two groups
with a facilitator in each group. With less than 24 players we have
the extra players standing around the outside of the zipper line of
spotters for extra support and spotting. We then rotate spotters with
each toss to keep players engaged – and to give the catchers a
rest.) Eskimo Toss is set up the same as Cookie Machine described
above (please review for set up). The one addition to the set up is
that one of the spotting players must move around to the head of the

active participant and be responsible for supporting the head at all times. The Eskimo toss also has a bit more energy involved so you can present it accordingly. Once the active participant is in the arms of the spotters, the idea here is that the spotters will be tossing the participant into the air (see the picture). It will be very important for the participant to keep her body "stiff as a board" during the toss – bending at the waist could allow the participant to "slip" through the arms of the spotters. The toss will also need to be synchronized by the spotters. When ready, the spotters count together, "1, 2, 3, toss" lifting arms together to toss up the participant. The spotters also need to be mindful to "catch with their legs," absorbing the weight by bending their knees, instead of catching with their backs. We like to instruct the group to start with a small toss – about spotter's eye level, progress to a medium toss – about head level, and then to a higher toss – just above the head level of the spotters, if the active participant is "up" for it (get it?) As always, you, as the facilitator, need to keep the actions safe. Also, we (the facilitators) should position ourselves near the head and shoulders of the player being tossed so we can put a hand in there if needed. When the tossing is complete make sure the spotters set the participant down feet first. The spotters at the shoulders and head safely set the participant up to standing. From here the groups can switch around so another player can be tossed. **Variations:** If you ever get the chance to experience the Eskimo Toss in an authentic blanket take it!!

Human Web You'll need a mid-size open area for this one. Plays well with groups of 12 to 14 (multiple groups can play if there is a facilitator with each group) for 30 to 40 minutes.

Process: The Human Web is a no-prop variation of the traditional Spiders Web activity - the same rules/safety issues apply. For this no-prop variation group members will be creating the holes the players will go through. Before you begin this activity sufficient practice with lifting and spotting should be done. More often than not we progress through Trio Trust Lean, the Cookie Machine, and Touching the Sky before we go into a Web activity. This gives our groups the skills they need to lift and pass along a participant safely if needed. If you are satisfied with the spotting safety skills of the group you can move into the Human Web. Ask your group to first decide how many low, middle and high holes their web will have – there should be one hole for every player who decides to go through the web. This is a great opportunity to use consensus building skills and also allows players to ask for what they want - exercising choice. When the number and levels of holes are chosen the group can begin. Each hole used will be created by two players joining hands to form a "vertical" circle. So, for example: low holes will be about knee high, middle holes will be waist high, and high holes will be head high. The players not forming the hole will be spotters for the player going through the hole, using all the safe spotting skills they have put into practice during other activities. The activity continues as participants progressively move through the holes they agreed to use. During this variation of the Web, we do not penalize players for touching any part of the Web (in this case the players forming the web). We use the Human Web to build trust and support with our groups – no penalties or consequences, just safe practices and helping behaviors. (Later on in the program we might progress to the traditional variation of the spiders web to add more challenge – they would then have to add the mental awareness to the physical skills they have already used and practiced.) **Variations:** You might require that no two people can form more than one hole together and/or that everyone must help in forming a hole at some point, thus different size & heights make for an almost endless variation of openings. Also, you might not require that the holes be "vertical" – you could just say they need to have enough holes for everyone in the group to go through. You might also limit the number of holes at each level.

Caterpillar Pass (this one is a variation, in height, to Body Surfing introduced by the New Games players) You'll want a mid-size open area. Plays well with 25 (or more) for about 30 to 45 minutes.

Process: First you will need to explain the activity (with the information provided below) so you can get a volunteer to be the initial active participant – the player to be passed. (You will also want to know who does not feel comfortable enough to be a passer – these players can be standing spotters.) Then you need to ask 4 other players to be standing spotters. From here you will ask the remainder of the group to form two lines facing each other – we like at least 10 players on each side. Have these players on their backs lying "ear-to-ear" with the person across from them, sort of like the "zipper" in Cookie Machine arrangement except now their entire body is the zipper instead of just their arms. At this point the players lying down (the passers) raise both arms straight up from the ground in

71

front of their face. This will look much like a huge "caterpillar" lying on its back with its legs sticking straight up!! When the passers are ready the standing spotters, two or more on each side of the active participant, help get the participant into a horizontal position as performed in Touching the Sky. From here the standing spotters pass the active participant (using their skills from Cookie Machine and the Human Web) onto the hands of the passing spotters lying on the floor (see picture for the visual). The passing spotters will of course need strong arms, being able to bend at the elbows, as they pass the active participant slowly down the line. As the player is being passed along the standing spotters move to the other end of the line to spot and lift the active participant off the passing hands – being very careful not to let the legs of the active participant kick any of the passers. **WARNING:** Needless to say (but we want to anyway) this activity has safety issues. You must be very diligent as a facilitator to keep things as safe as possible. Make sure there are enough players helping to lift and pass the active participant – before, during, and after. Keep the activity slow and controlled. You, or other standing spotters, will be able to step in around the line (watch out for stepping on hair) to help support along the way if needed. Above all, be mindful of your group. If you have any apprehensions you might choose another activity. We don't want you to avoid this activity – it is very powerful. We just want you to "Keep'em safe!"

Caveat: The remaining activities in this section we consider to be the most "risky," first physically and then emotionally (if the physically isn't taken care of!). We do pride ourselves on safely monitoring our groups and at the same time giving the groups space enough to feel it is their own experience. However, we tend to be much more involved and methodical about these last two. Take the steps slowly and make sure everyone in your group understands what they are doing and what they are asked to do next before each step of the activity.

Lap Lounging (passed along to us by Craig Dobkin) You'll need an area large enough for half of your group to make a mid-size circle. Plays well with 24 (or more) for 25 to 35 minutes.

Process: (This one is a bit wordy, but well worth the time.) Before we even start to explain this activity we will first invite the group to participate in a more "intimate" activity (right away you might sense that even asking this question is only for certain groups – you are right). By intimate, we explain that they will be in close contact with each other – within each others' personal space. We also remind them that there is always a choice within the activity that will allow a participant to be involved in a less intimate way. If the group agrees we move ahead with the explanation. The overall concept is that players will be lying in the lap of a player behind them in a half sitting half lying configuration (stick with us here). The formation of this activity is a circle so each player will be lying in a lap and their own lap will be laid upon (see the picture's included). The set up of this goes in methodical stages. Ask players to pair up with someone close to their height and weight (if there are an odd number of players we can usually work the extra person into the second Lounging opportunity with a player whose partner does not care to Lounge). One of the partners is going to be the lounger the other will be the spotter. Have the loungers form a Double Chicken Wing circle (see

The Chicken Game in Frontloaders) and then turn to their right (just make sure all the loungers are facing the same direction). At this point you, the facilitator, might need to rearrange some players. You want to avoid extreme variations in size among players who are next to each other, e.g., the tallest player is standing behind the shortest

player. Variations in height are not an issue; just get a nice flow of short to tall. (Some of you might be noticing that the set up is like the traditional Lap Sit activity – true, but we're not going to "sit" on laps.) At this point the spotters come in. Spotters will be kneeling down to the outside of their partner, slightly behind them, on their right knee and placing their left leg up as a seat for their partner. (It has been suggested that if you have something available to kneel on to provide some cushion for the knee, it is very helpful. If you are able to perform the lounge outside in the grass you can have some natural cushion.) The loungers then sit down, carefully, on their partner's leg. Before moving ahead the position of the players might need adjustment. Each seated lounger will need to have the small of their back (or seat area) as close to the knees of the player behind them as possible – not sitting on any part of the player behind. You will also want to make sure the shape of the circle is round!!! So, adjust away (this tends to be when the spotters' knees take a beating). When the group is nice and round, seats to knees, they are ready for a lounge. Together, usually on a count of 1, 2, 3, the loungers slowly lie back into the lap of the player behind them. Each spotter can use their hands and arms to support their partners reclining. Here they have reached the "intimate" point. As the facilitator, help the group/loungers adjust their positions enough so that they all feel comfortable and supported by the player behind them, because, we're not done yet. The loungers are all going to arch their backs up, by pushing off their feet and squeezing their glutes together, enough so that their spotter/partners can remove her or his leg. Spotters must bring their leg out by PULLING THEIR LEFT FOOT BACK TOWARDS THEM and then taking out their leg. DO NOT push the left foot into the middle of the circle and then take the leg out (if their partner where to fall to the ground the spotter's leg would be in a bad position!) Please review the extraction again. All the while the

spotters are removing their legs they should be keeping hand contact with their partner in a way that provides some stabilization – lower back and shoulder areas. Once the leg of the spotter is out, the lounger can relax – un-arch their back – into the lap they are in. The physics here is the weight of each player is distributed through the entire area of the lounge contact of the circle. When all the spotter's legs are out and the circle of loungers has stabilized, have the spotters give the loungers a little room so they can feel their independence – spotters should be close by however! It is a pretty remarkable feeling to be within the lounging circle. It is also just as remarkable to observe the structure of players. After a few moments of revelation the process needs to be reversed. Spotters get ready at the side of their partners. Loungers need to arch back up enough so their partner can get their leg back under for support. When all the spotters are back in place you can call a "1, 2, 3," before the loungers slowly sit back up – spotters supporting them during the incline. After the celebration of the accomplishment, switch roles so the spotters can now take a lounge. **Note:** Again, be mindful of safety every step of the way. Check in with spotters – they are taking most of the physical risk. Check in with loungers to make sure they feel stable before removing their spotters. Make sure the structure of the circle is sound. These precautions don't take long, so make sure you take the time! Have fun with it!

Gyroscope (variation of Perfect Entry shared by Karl Rohnke) You'll need a small open space for every group of 8 to 10 players that you have – if you have several groups you'll need a nice open area. Plays well with 8 to 25 for 30 to 40 minutes.

Process: As mentioned in the caveat above, be mindful of the safety needs of this activity. Take one step at a time making sure everyone understands their responsibility at each step. If you have 16 or more players you can create smaller groups of at least 8 people.

We do not require that you have a facilitator with each group because groups will only Gyroscope players when you are with that particular group. The overall idea is that the group will be turning (Gyroscoping) one of their members around 360 degrees – head-over-heels. Planning the process is the most critical part of the activity. One player will volunteer to be Gyroscoped – he stands in the center of the group. His responsibility during the activity is to keep completely stiff-as-a-board during the gyro process – just like in Trio Trust Lean and Touching the Sky above. The remainder of the group (with constant check in with the player they are gyroscoping) plans how they are going to lift this player up, turn him around, where at some point he will be upside-down, and then continue the turning until he is placed back on his feet again. The action cannot be performed in any way until the facilitator approves it. The facilitator will be asking for the overall plan and then specific information from each player about what they are going to be doing during the activity – describing every step they are going to take from the time the player is lifted from the ground to the time he is set back onto the ground. If the facilitator does not need to make changes, for safety reasons, and the participant that is being gyroscoped agrees with the plan, the group is allowed to perform the gyroscope. The facilitator stays with the group to monitor their actions and assist them if needed. If there are other groups still working on their plan, they can continue their process or observe another group performing the Gyroscope. Remember, groups cannot implement their plan until it is approved by the facilitator at which point the facilitator stays with the group for supervision. After a rouse of celebration, groups rotate players so another person can be gyroscoped. Most groups we have seen, implement the same plan on another player, however, there have been times where the plan is adapted for a given reason. In any case, the same steps must be followed, as above, for each player that is gyroscoped. **Variations:** An interesting challenge can be added to this activity. Have the player being gyroscoped hold onto a glass of water – how full is up to the players (see pictures).

"If it has been too long, it has!"

Challenges & Problem Solving

The following activities build upon a foundation the group has created up to this point. They have gotten to know each other (and themselves) enough to play together and have some fun; they've gained some knowledge and practice with communicating, and hopefully have developed some skills that will help them communicate even better as the activities become more challenging. And, they have also participated in activities that have built trust and confidence in their abilities together and as individuals. The activities in this section are best attempted with a good level of trust - trust in one-self and others; Trust enough to take more personal and group risks without the fear of failure. Most of the activities that follow will require players to think beyond what is apparent. Other activities just require good old listening, sharing and doing, but without trust in each other the activities would be difficult to accomplish. Remember, all activities are meant to be built upon each other using information from one to help in another - in other words, practicing the skills needed to be successful within a group. Also, keep in mind, it is okay to go back to other types of activities or a Fun Filled Game from time-to-time for a "mental" break. Fun is a very important factor in keeping players engaged in the process. As a reminder, these activities are in no particular order of challenge - one group's challenge is another group's walk in the park.

The Clapper (shared by an adventure colleague) You don't need much space for this one because there is very little movement required. Plays well with 2 to 25 (or more) for 10 to 15 minutes.

Process: This activity is involves getting the entire group to clap together at the same time – making only "one" clapping sound. The journey of this activity is where the challenge lies. The group needs to

81

coordinate their efforts to create that one sound. They will also have to decide if the sound they have made is indeed one together – without other sounds (claps) coming in before or after. Once the group has worked out their process to create just one sound (clap), challenge them to see how many "one sound" claps they can do in a row. This might become rhythmical in nature – 1, 2, 3, clap, 1, 2, 3, clap, or just random coordination. We find this one to be a quick challenge our groups seem to get into – appealing to the three major learning styles. **Variations:** You could also try a foot stomp or challenge the group to use a vocal noise of some sort like, "Hey" or "Oh" or "Tee."

Human Warp (variation of a Karl Rohnke activity) You'll need enough room for your group to create a comfortable circle. Plays well with 10 to 25 players for 20 to 30 minutes.

Process: We discovered a fun prop-less way to present the traditional Group Juggle activity. Call for a Double Chicken Wing circle (see The Chicken Game in Frontloaders). Ask the group to establish an "order" to pass a clap around through the group. We help this process by first asking someone (player 1) to start out by pointing to someone across the circle from them (player 2) – not at someone next to them. Player 2 points to a different player (player 3). Player 3 points to a player 4 and so on until the last player pointed to points at player 1 – each player points to one player and each player is only pointed at once. After this "order" has been created, challenge the group to pass a clap through the order as fast as they can (you might like to use a stopwatch if this helps to motivate the group. If you ask a group member to time the activity would this one still be a prop-less? Hey, *you* didn't have to bring anything!). Here is where the facilitator comes in. We tend to use this activity in the context of "outside assessment." Many situations in the "real world" are monitored by an outside influence like a parent, a boss, or a customer. So, in this case the facilitator will be regulating the claps. The guidelines that will be monitored are, 1) no two players can be clapping at the same time and 2) each player must perform a clap – the claps must be non-simultaneous, performed in sequence through the established order. In other words if there are 20 players in your group you need to hear 20 different claps – each player making a clap keeping with the established order. We stick with this one as long as the energy is good. You could then move into the infamous Warp Speed type of activity. Challenge the group to some unbelievably low time, say 5 seconds. If they were to think "out-of-the-box" as we say, they could achieve the time by moving and standing next to the player they are passing their clap to, keeping the same "order," thus more able to coordinate claps. **Note:** Use your best judgment as to when and how to present the challenges here. **Variations:** Take out the claps and use this process with Pass Your Own Name Game found in the Icebreakers.

Shoe Find (around since the shoe!) You'll need a nice open area. Plays well with 12 to 25 or more for 20 to 25 minutes. (This one was on the borderline of prop and prop-less, but since you don't have to bring anything....we decided to add it.)

Process: Everyone picks a partner (a group of 3 can work). Without further explanation have them visually examine the shoes of their partner(s). One partner is to become the "communicator", the other partner is to become the "extractor." Inside a designated area (like the inside of a big circle made by the group) have the extractor leave one or both of her shoes – leave both if you have more time to play. Both partners then retreat back to the big circle some distance away from the shoes. Before play begins you'll want to thoroughly mix up the pile of shoes. The communicator remains sighted but must remain behind the designated circle area. The "extractor" closes her eyes and keeps them closed. Using voice commands, the communicator directs the extractor back to the area where the extractor must extract her own shoe(s) and then return to the designated line. Once all the extractors have found their own shoes they switch roles with the communicators – the communicators now become the extractors. **Variation:** Another fun shoe activity: Have all the players toss their shoes into a big pile then each player takes one right and one left shoe – not their own shoe or a matching pair. Holding the left shoe in their right hand and the right shoe in their left hand, players match up shoes so they end up in one large circle of paired shoes. At this point all the players set the shoes down and everyone goes to their shoes to reunite – don't forget to meet everyone you stand next to. This can be done a few times to randomly meet other players.

Line up According to the Number (shared by Neil Mercer) You need a mid-size open area for this one. Plays well with 20 to 25 (or more) for 15 to 18 minutes.

Process: The challenge of this activity is in "the eye of the beholder" since it's very, as Neil puts it, ambiguous and open ended. The risk here is the level of "letting go" and being silly. We like to use it to see where the players are at with each other – what their level of "play-ablity" is. We have also used this one to decide where we want to take the group next. With all that said, all you tell your group is

"Line up according to the Number." What Number? How to line up? The conundrum begins. Short (generally) and sweet. A variety of possibilities can ensue. You might get those, "What are you talking about" looks, you might see complete engagement, you might see a little of both. We have offered a few responses in the past, like, "You have all the information you need within your group." Or "How fun do you want to make it?" - the sort of information players just love to hear from us. We also tend to use this one several times during a program to see how it evolves. **Variations:** Dr. Christian Itin suggests having the group do this one without talking.

Mono-Pod (shared with us by Karl Rohnke, right after he tried it for the first time on an unsuspecting group he was working with) You'll need enough room for your group to make a circle.

Plays well with 8 to 25 (or more) for 10 to 15 minutes.

Process: Mono-Pod requires a bit of leg strength, actually, single leg strength. So, we tend to plan this one with groups who are a bit more interested in the physical parts of the challenges. Circle up your group and have

85

them hold hands (this can change if the group sees fit to do so). Ask the players to then support themselves by standing on their strongest leg. Have them put their free leg up into the center of the circle – it just needs to be off the ground. The challenge for the group, while keeping in contact with each other, is for all players to squat down together on the support leg as far as possible (the ultimate is sitting on the support heel) and then stand back up together without touching the ground with any other parts of their bodies – the tough "part" is the other leg. We allow the group to plan any strategy that will fit the parameters – the players in constant contact and only a single foot from each player touching the ground. **WARNING:** There is the safety risk of falling over so make the players aware of supporting each other as much as possible. Also, if there are players that are concerned about their knee strength, invite them to help spot the group – a very important role! **Variations:** You could try this one first with small groups then combine groups to see how the dynamics change.

Letter-add-it (variation of a Karl Rohnke activity). You won't need much open room for this one since there's no running – so just some hanging around space. Works well with 12 to 25 for 10 to 15 minutes.

Process: Have your group standing/sitting in random positions – avoid any sort of a circle. The objective (challenge) for the group is to call out the alphabet (English A, B, Cs) in sequence without any two players calling the same letter at the same time. This is a random activity where no planning is allowed, just a "go-for-it" challenge. The only other rule is that players cannot make eye contact with each other during the process. To get the game started (at any time during a program), we will call out, "A!" nice and loud. At this point the challenge is on. Any time two (or more) players call out the same letter or we see players making eye contact with each other, we call out, "A!" again real loud – this indicates a restart due to a violation of the challenge. We usually will not spend any more than 15 minutes on this one since the energy seems to die down after a while. We'll transition into another activity after the group has beaten their best (highest) letter. This intermediate success motivates the group to revisit the challenge again later. And when they get it, A to Z don't forget the celebrate! **Variations:** Take out the "no eye contact" rule and see how they communicate – still no planning allowed. The original activity involves using numbers. If there are 21 players in your group (including you) you use 21 numbers – the facilitator calling out, "ONE!" to start and restart. Along with the numbers is a great "math" challenge. Once the group is successful with the challenge (counted 1 through 21) everyone keeps the number they called. At random one player will call her number – if two players call out at the same time the facilitator calls, "restart." After a single number is called the facilitator calls a mathematical action like, add, subtract, divide, or multiply. Another player can then shout out his number to add to the equation. The answer must be called out within the group – by either one or two players, i.e., "two" and "five" could be combined to form the number "25".

Virtual Juggle (learned, mostly, from Sam Sikes) You'll need a nice open space for your group to form a circle. Plays well with 16 to 25 players for 25 to 35 minutes.

Process: Ask the group to form a Double Chicken Wing circle (see The Chicken Game in Frontloaders). Ask each player to hold up one hand. Establish a pattern by taking turns at pointing and saying "you" to someone across the circle (just like in the activity Human Warp found in this section). After a player has pointed he or she should put his or her hand down – the last player pointed to will point to the first player that pointed. Have the group practice the, "You Pattern" until they have it down. Now you are going to ask the group to establish a, "Fruit and Vegetable Pattern" different from the, "You Pattern." So, same process, have players hold up one hand. Have one player start by pointing to someone across the circle saying a fruit or vegetable (make sure you remind the players to remember the fruit or vegetable that was passed to them and the one they passed). After pointing the player puts down his hand. Ask players not to repeat any fruits and/or vegetables – 25 players 25 different fruits or vegetables. Have the group practice this one several times so they can get it into memory. Then ask them to close their eyes and repeat the fruit and vegetable pattern – they will be a bit surprised, but will soon realize it's doable. The interesting aspect of this activity is that it combines the use of all three major learning styles into one activity. The "You Pattern" requires the visual and the "Fruit and Vegetable Pattern" requires the auditory (as you proved by having the group close their eyes). What remains is the kinesthetic learning style. Here's where the activity gets interesting. Practice the "You Pattern" once again. Along with this pattern the players will be moving to the spot of the person they are passing the "You" to. For example, if I'm passing my "You" to Scott, I point at Scott and say, "You" while I'm walking towards him. Scott needs to move from his spot, in the direction of the person he points to in the "You Pattern," before I reach Scott's spot – which then becomes my new place in the circle. Scott is on his way to his new place in the circle after his "You" player vacates her spot. The most challenging part of this activity for the players seems to be remembering that they only move from their spot during the "You Pattern," because, after sufficient practice moving during the "You Pattern" they are going to add their "Fruit and Vegetable Pattern." So, as the "You Pattern" is going on (with "Yous" and movements) a designated player is going to start out the "Fruit and Vegetable Pattern" by calling out her food real loud, "Apple!" The next player, remembering that an apple was passed to him, calls out his, "Tomato!" and the pattern continues – at the same time the "You Pattern" is going on. If the "Fruit and Vegetable Pattern" dies out, any player can start it up again calling out his or her food. We usually challenge the group to success by getting through the "Fruit and Vegetable Pattern" twice without a break in the flow. Don't be apprehensive about stopping and regrouping. Find out from the group where the challenges are, practice what is needed, then give it another try. We have rarely seen groups just breeze right through this one. However, when they get it, it sure is rewarding. **Note:** If you see fit, you might need to remind the group that this activity is not being timed – you'll see what we mean.

*"Monkeys see, monkeys doo, so.....
watch where you step!"*

Closings

The activities in this section are used to tie things together after a large block of community building activities or after a full day of programming. They are meant to provide time for participants to reflect on what they have learned and what they might have accomplished during their adventure experience. Closings can be very serious or light and fun - you need to decide what is best for the group and their purpose for being together. How would you like to see them go home? What would you like them to remember? What will they pass along to their family and friends about the day? Closings give the experience an anchor. And like all anchors they must be pulled up so the ship can move on. But the anchor is always there when needed.

Group Hug! (we think this one's been around since the Hug!) You'll need enough room for your group to make a circle. Works well with 2 to 25 (or more) for 4 to 6 minutes.

Process: Ask the group to get into a Chicken Soup circle (see The Chicken Game in Frontloaders) Have them place their arms around the shoulders or waists of the players to either side. Then scoot a bit forward until the group is "hip-to-hip". We tell them, "This is a nice hug, but we can do better!" Have the group lift their right leg and point it into the middle of the circle. On "1, 2, 3," the whole group is asked to step forward with their right leg giving each other in the circle a nice BIG hug all at the same time! Great for a "no-time-left" closing for the day!! **Note:** Be mindful of players who might "overdo" it a bit - as always, the right activity for the right group at the right time. **Variations:** If there is time, it's always great to get a hug or a handshake from everyone before they go – brightens up everyone's day!

Digital Contract (revisited) (variation of the Five Finger Contract presented by Laurie Frank) You only need sitting around room for this one. Works well with 10 to 25 for 10 to 25 minutes.

Process: The Digital Contract that was presented in the Frontloaders section can also be used as a closing. Revisit what each of the digits on your hand represented and have the group give you specific examples that occurred during the day that addressed each of the concepts. Expand on any of the points that seem to stir up interest. This process and review can be used along with other Closings.

Just One Word (this one was shared by Jim Cain found in, *Teamwork and Teamplay*) You just need "sitting around" space. Works well with 6 to 25 players for 15 to 30 minutes.

Process: This is a nice frontloaded closing (or debrief) that is not too threatening. If the opportunity arises, you can try to expand on the participant's answers. Have the players in the group complete any (or all) of the following phrases with a single word answer:

> I began the day feeling…
> The first time I was challenged I felt…
> I felt _____ by the rest of the group.
> Right now I feel…
> What I'll remember most about the day is…

Depending on the size of the group and the time we have will determine the number of questions we can ask. Don't forget to remind the group members that it is okay to pass if they do not want to share – they are still thinking about it (processing it) in their heads. And again, if the opportunity presents itself, you could go a little deeper with some of the questions. If you decide to go deeper, make sure there is enough time to address what comes out. **Variations:** Another powerful sharing along this line is to ask a question that the participants can answer using only their hands – making symbols and shapes. This is most appropriate when involved in a very reflective closing.

Well Oiled Machine (shared by Michelle Cummings of *Training Wheels*) You'll need enough room for your group to end up in a circle. Plays well with 6 to 25 for 10 to 20 minutes.

Process: This is a fun, creative way to end the day. After your group has worked well together all day long, "like a well oiled machine", have them take that home with them. Explain to them that groups and companies have all kinds of parts that make them work, much like a car engine. Without the smallest part, the machine is ineffective. Instruct them to think of a noise and an action in their head. Ask for one volunteer to start out doing their action and noise (example, someone may pretend to turn a crank on a car and make a grinding noise.) Then after the first person has performed his/her action for about 5 seconds, another person connects somewhere to the first person and comes up with a new action and a new noise. One at a time the rest of the group will enter the circle, attach to the machine already in process and add their noise and action. By the time everyone has joined the machine it will be whistling and bustling about with activity. A fun way to end the day!

Virtual Postcards (learned way-back-when, we wish we knew who to credit for this one – help us out if you can) You just need "sitting around" space. Works well with 6 to 25 players for 15 to 35 minutes.

Process: At the conclusion of the program day ask each participant to create a virtual postcard. Have them choose a picture for the front, something that they would like to pass along to someone else (some people like to do those split postcards with a couple pictures). Then on the back indicate who you are going to send it to and what you will say to the person with the space available (4 inch by 6 inch postcard). After giving the group some contemplation time, go around and have them share their postcard with the group if they choose. **Variations:** There is a similar activity in, *Reflective Learning* where the participants review the day with the facilitator as if they were watching a film. Then, from that film they each choose a picture they would like to "cut out," frame, and hang on their wall. They also are asked to share what this picture will remind them of. (*Reflective Learning* has a number of other no-prop types of debriefing activities.)

Circle of Friends (shared by Matt Weinstein, found in, *99 of the best Experiential Corporate Games we Know*). You'll need enough room to make a circle with your group. Works well with 10 to 25 players for 10 to 20 minutes.

Process: Have the group form a Chicken Soup circle (see The Chicken Game in Frontloaders). Place their arms around the shoulder or waist of the person on either side. Explain that the circle will move to the "left" by taking tiny baby steps. If someone would like to stop the circle and share with the group about their thoughts or feelings about the day, then they yell out "STOP!" Once they have shared, they say, "move to the right." The circle moves, taking small steps, to the right until another player who wants to share calls out "STOP!" again. When this player is finished sharing he calls out, "left" and the circle moves to the left. This process continues to the left and right until all those who wish to participate have been given the opportunity to speak up. When the facilitator "feels" that it's time (the group is still moving), she or he will start a countdown from 10 to 1. In that time if someone says, "Stop!" the process continues. Another countdown is given when it "feels" right again. If the facilitator reaches "one" the activity concludes.

Note: Moving together as a group, taking small steps, gives the group something to do during the (sometimes) awkward times of silence. Ending Circle of Friends with a "Group Hug" listed above is a great way to end any day!!

"There is a time and place for everything under the sun, so don't forget your sunscreen!"

Vortex with a Twist (learned from Sam Sikes). You'll need enough room to form a circle with your group. Works well with 10 to 25 players for 12 to 20 minutes.

Process: Ask the group to form a Double Chicken Wing circle (see The Chicken Game in Frontloaders) and then hold hands.

As the facilitator, join the circle between two players. You then break hands with one of the people to your side while asking the participants to continue holding hands, but to follow your lead!? You then turn, face-to-face with the person whom you are still holding hands with and give them a compliment for the day. After giving a compliment to the first player move to the second player and give her a compliment, taking that first person with you as you go. Moving to the third person, you give a compliment while the player you are holding hands with is giving a compliment to the second player. As you move to the fourth person, the person next to you is now facing the third person and they are to commend each other on the day. As you move around the circle players are giving compliments to the players they are facing. Continuing the movement you eventually turn the circle inside out and rejoin hands with the other end of the circle. Sam says, "Now it's time to take what we learned or experienced here and to transfer it back to the outside world we will return to." Finally, ask your group,

without letting go of hands, to turn and face back into the middle of the circle. "What do we see?" Sam asks. Here is the opportunity for participants to reflect on the day - still holding hands. Sam concludes, "Regardless of where we go next, this experience has brought us closer together." At this point the group can drop hands and share any parting celebrations.

Celebration Circle (shared by Faith Evans) You'll need a nice open area for this one. Plays well with 15 to 25 players for 25 to 30 minutes.
Process: At the close of your program split your group into smaller groups of 3 to 5 players. Have each group work independently for 10 minutes designing a celebration that will fit the end of the day and that can be taught in a single demonstration to the other

groups. You want to emphasize that the theme of celebration might be to identify and commemorate what was learned that may include powerful insights, humorous episodes, significant events, or specific valuable lessons. Qualify that the celebration should be short, vivid, specific, and inclusive (meaning everyone is able to repeat it). After 10 minutes gather the groups together and form a Double Chicken Wing circle (see The Chicken Game in Frontloaders) keeping the small group members together around the circle. Indicate to each group when they will perform their celebration – give out the order. Then each group, from their position in the circle, will enthusiastically present their celebration for everyone else to observe. Then they will immediately present it in a way that everyone else can learn it. Finally, everyone in the circle repeats the celebration together – present the celebration, teach it, then everyone does it together. After a round of applause, the next group begins the same process. **Note:** Ms. Evans encourages us to keep the energy and participation high by establishing the pace – keep moving quickly and intentionally from group to group until everyone is finished. Don't permit pauses to dull the excitement. **Variations:** If the energy is still going, perform one final round repeating each celebration in order without any pauses. End with high fives all around.

"Fortune is in the eye of the beholder."

Fun Filled Games

This section includes a variety of activities that can be used as fillers, energizers and competitive experiences. When we use these activities we usually don't process them but we do take the time to emphasize that playing with and against other players is as much about community-building as any other activity. If we can teach compassion, respect and fairness within the context of competition, our outlook of it can change for the better. HAVE FUN!

Eye Contact Partner Tag (ECPT) (shared by Patrick Gallagher) You'll need a mid-size open space for your group to run around in. Plays well with 16 to 25 (or more) for 10 to 15 minutes.

Process: Have (or set up) every player with a partner. A group of three will work out if needed. Create a boundary area (using safe corner markers like coats or sweaters) suitable for your group size – the smaller the area the more interesting the game (the larger the area the more dangerous – faster running). This one plays like the historical Partner Tag where players use a simple hand tag to transfer the "IT." Also the only player you will be able to tag is your partner and after being tagged you must make two complete turns in place before proceeding to tag your partner back. All these same rules apply to ECPT however, the one big difference is the mode of tagging. To tag your partner you must make eye contact with her or him. With this in mind, there are a few additional rules. All players must keep their eyes open. Non-"IT" players must keep their open eyes (it's okay to blink) at head level – either making eye contact with another player or looking at some part of another players skull area. Finally, we like to play the no-contact rule. Players are not allowed to link up in any way with another person as to prevent another player access to possible eye contact. To start the game, decide which player will be "IT" first. The "ITs" stand in the center of the boundary area for a count of five (the group counting together) while the other players find strategic (?!) advantage within the playing area. We tend to play 60 second rounds. After 60 seconds the untagged partner is the winner of the round. ECPT is one of those games that is not done justice by the written word. Give it a try, it's really interesting. **Variations:** You might add the rule that players may not maintain eye contact with anyone for more than 3 seconds – adds a bit more "tagging" potential. We often progress into ECPT from the traditional tag version (Partner Tag) to keep the game and interest going. And if we may (props are involved), Chris' favorite Partner Tag variation is played with foam pool Noodles!

Flashback Tag You'll need a nice big open area to run around in. Plays well with 12 to 25 for 15 to 20 minutes.

Process: Flashback Tag can be set up as a fast walking game or free speed depending on your group. We also like to revisit the, "Bumpers Up" running position – arms up in front of the player's chest area, fingers up, palms facing away from the players body, and a little bend in the elbows. This position will do a couple things. It will slow the players down a bit – it's hard to run really fast with the arms up, and the hands and arms will be used to absorb some of the shock of another player's body if they come too close to each other. (And, in this game, the hands are ready for tagging.) During this Bumper practice, remind the players that you all want to be safe by watching out for each other during all the running around - avoid the "crashes." So, on with the game. This is a group tag game very similar to the infamous Everybody's IT but no one has to be out. Each player will be tagging other players to gain a score. A tag can only be done using an open hand touching the "back" (not the "back-side") of any other player in the group. Each time a player touches someone's back they get a point – keeping track of their own score.

100

Before starting, point out the boundary area. There really is no need to mark them because if players run to far from the action they will not be able to gain any points. Each round lasts for 30 seconds (or more if you like - we don't go beyond 60 seconds). The objective is for the players to get as many points as they can during each round. Players will end up with different scores in 30 seconds, this is great – diversity. Explain that there is no overall "winner." The idea will be to play several rounds and try to achieve a new personal best each time. When they are ready, give them the, "GO" and start the time. Give them a 10 second warning and then a 5 second count-down using the word, "FREEZE" to indicate that the time is up - to stop moving and tagging. Go around and ask them how they did, give them a little rest, challenge them to beat their personal best, and then start another round. **Variation:** To make Flashback Tag more competitive, first player to 10 points (or more) shouts, "TEN!" and the game is over. Rematches are bound to ensue.

Body Part Tag (one of the classics) You'll need a nice big area to run around in. Plays well with 12 to 25 players for 10 to 15 minutes.

Process: This one is a fun staple tag game we like to use to introduce the "challenge" concept. We have played this one as an elimination game or a point gathering game like Flashback Tag above. We have played with 1 or 2 players being IT or everybody being IT – we like all the flexible choices. Basically, when someone gets tagged they squat down (or move to the side) until the round is over (if it's a point gathering the player stays in). Players tag each other with an open hand. Our first round is usually a large body area like the back. After that round the next target is any part of either arm. Then we tag just one arm – right or left. Finally we move to tagging the hand – how will the players determine if they were tagged or if they tagged. The progressive challenge issue is one we can discuss after the game. This final round of tagging the hand is an interesting gauge of the players competitive nature – issues tend to surface here that can be added to the processing session. In any case, this has been a fun warm-up for us. **Variations:** Sean McFeely rekindled a nice addition to Body Part Tag. Playing with one or two "ITs", a tagged player must fall to the ground and wave their arms exclaiming "Help Me, Help Me!" Any four untagged players can help this person reenter the game by lifting him up (teamwork) by his four appendages and carrying him over the boundary line. The four helping players are immune to any tags. After crossing the boundary line all the players may go back into the game. It is also permissible for three, two, or even one person to carry (drag usually) the helpless player across the boundary line, but these helpers are still vulnerable to being tagged themselves. Once the taggers render any help possible the round is over – or you can call a countdown if the energy is fading.

Eye Tag (picked up at a conference, please help if you know the source). You just need enough room to circle up your group. Plays well with 12 to 25 for 15 to 20 minutes.

Process: Eye Tag is a blatant out-right elimination game that most players just love to play over and over – they want to be one of the last standing. Form a Double Chicken Wing circle (see The Chicken Game in Frontloaders). Then have all the players look down at the floor or ground. As the facilitator you will do the calls. When you say, "Ready? Look up," the players all look up at the same time. Each player must look up at one other player (no looking around) in the circle as if they wanted to make eye contact with this player. However, if eye contact is made both players are out of the game. After the reactions and readjusting the circle after any players leave, you call, "Look down." When everyone is ready, repeat, "Ready? Look up." Continue this process until the group is weeded out to 2, 1, or even no players. Then, circle back up for another round. **Variations:** For a faster version, any players that make eye contact stay in the game. Add the rule that a player cannot look at the same person twice in a row – you know those planners!

Slow Tag (learned from Sam Sikes) You'll need a nice big open area to run around in. Plays well with 12 to 25 for 10 to 12 minutes.

Process: We do like to mark the four corners of our boundary area for this one with something soft like coats or sweaters. Make a good size boundary to fit the size of your group. Ask everyone to get their own personal space within the boundary – no one should be able to touch anyone at this point. Being that this is a tag game, if you get tagged with an open hand anywhere (or limit the spot like in Body Part Tag above) on the body you must sit down. During the game the leader will call, "Step" at which point each player can take one step – one foot in any direction (if the other foot moves from the spot where it is at, the player has to sit). The leader calls, "Step" again. Now the other foot can take a step in any direction. The only time a player can move is when the facilitator calls, "STEP!" There will be some interesting tactics developed during this game. Again, after you are tagged you sit down, however, you are not out of the

game. The sitting players become, as Karl Rohnke has so dubbed them, "Ankle Biters" and can still tag others who are moving about. Players must be in the SITTING position (how ever this is defined at the beginning of the game) and they are not allowed to tag the player who tagged them. Play until there are two people left – or go for the duel. Whatever you have time for.

Random-alities (from the adventure-based commu-nity) You'll need a mid-size open area. Plays well with 16 to 25 (or more) for 15 to 25 minutes.

Process: Random-alities can be done cooperatively in small groups (similar to Birthday Line-Up found in the Ice-Breakers section) just to emphasize small group communication and par-ticipation or you can put a little competition in the game to charge things up a bit. Randomly form groups of 8 to10 people. Our ideal structure is using 2 or 3 groups (no less than 8 in a group). If there are an odd number of players one line will have an additional person to work with – who said life was fair? Position the groups so they will be in front of you. You will be calling out a random trait like, tallest to shortest. Each group independently will line up single file in this order. When they are done each player in the group must raise one arm/hand up and together with their teammates yell, "DONE!" You, as the facilitator, must decide if the groups are coordinated in their effort to be, "DONE!" We're not easy on them. They must have a coordinated finish to count for a medal. Metaphorically hand out the Gold, Silver, and Bronze medals as teams finish – you might need to verify the order of some groups based on their out-of-the-box thinking habits. When ready, give the groups another trait to line up in. Continue play until the energy starts to subside. **Variations:** Mix teams up each time – how does this change the dynamics? You could also put everyone back together again into one team and do line-ups for speed. What process can they develop to improve their time. Other traits might include (see Birthday Line-Up for a few more) shoe size, number of siblings, number of freckles, shade of hair, lightest to darkest skin color, total of their social security number, age, number of fillings, alphabetical after spelling their name backwards, length of hair, etc..

The Captain's Coming Back for More (a couple variations of a classic) You'll need a nice big open area. This one works best with 20 or more players for 15 to 20 minutes.

Process: This little warm-up game has been a staple item for many game leaders. It is meant to be presented with enthusiastic energy and animation. First you will need to teach all the actions that are described below. In the traditional version, *The Captains On Deck* is a single person saluting, *Swab the Deck* is a single person mopping around, *Lighthouse* is two players connecting hands overhead, turning around beeping. *Man Overboard* is three players, two are holding hands to form a circle the third player inside looking over the side of the boat. *Row Ashore* is four players in a single file line rowing (not paddling) a boat. *Grub Time* is five people in a tight circle pretending to eat saying, "grub, grub, grub…" and *All Hands on Deck* brings all the players back into the game.

Below there are two other themes you could go with, or make up one related to your program. After the group has practiced the formations a bit, inform them that you will be calling out the formations in a random sequence. If a player or players are not able to get into the correct number group or there are too many, or too few, players in one group doing the action, the player or players are sent off to the sidelines of the game to sing a theme related song. In the traditional theme the players sing, "Oh, EE, Oh, a pirates life for me, Oh, EE, Oh, a pirates life for me" continuing until they hear "All Hands on Deck" or the game has ended. Again, presented with energy and a sprinkle of fun, the players should be moving around and singing not even realizing the silly chaos.

The Chief is Here (be sensitive and respectful to cultural issues when presenting this version)

"*The Chief is Here*" – 1 person: arms across chest, standing still with very proud look on their face.

"*Indian Wrestle*" - 2 people: face each other outsides of their right feet touching, clasp right hands and pretend to pull each other off balance.

"*Smoke Signals*" – 3 people: making a small circle move straight arms up and down over the "fire" sending out smoke signals.

"*Scouting Party*" – 4 people: in a single file line, right hand on the shoulder of the player in front, left hand over the eyebrows looking for game (galloping around the area is optional).

"*Teepee*" – 5 people: one sitting on the floor "Indian style" with other 4 holding their hands up over the head of the sitting person to form a teepee.

If a player or players cannot get into the correct groupings they go off to the side and sing, "Home, home on the range, where the deer and the antelope play. Home, home, on the range…." The facilitator can call "Tribal Meeting" to call everyone back into the game.

Christ is Here!

"*Christ is Here*" – 1 person: head bowed in prayer.

"*Light Unto The World*" – 2 people: back to back acting like a light house beacon.

" *Fisher of Men*" – 3 people: join hands around a third person. Person in the middle is casting for fish.

"*Four Horseman of the Apocalypse*" – 4 people: next to each other like they are riding horses together.

"*The Wedding Feast*" – 5 people: eating around a table.

If you can not form the "appropriate" activity then go to Heaven and start singing "Amazing Grace". The facilitator can call, "*Revival*" to bring everyone back into the game.

Two Truths and a Fib (or Two) (traditional party game). You just need some sitting around room. Works well with 8 to 25 for 15 to 25 minutes.

Process: If you have a large group of players you might want to make 2 groups. This involves a little "creative" story telling that seems to work better with the older participants. But, don't let it stop you. When your group is sitting around have someone share three (real) short stories or statements about themselves. Two of these stories or statements must be true, one is not. After the statements, go around to each player and find out which statement they thing is the fib. After everyone has made their vote the fibber can share the fib. A fun way to get to know each other a little better.

Variations: When working with younger groups we suggest that their fib could be a true story with a different ending. Go for Two Fibs and the Truth. This activity is a good way to open the topic of not telling the truth and the effects it has.

Egg-olution (ERPS) (shared by Mike Spiller). You need a mid-size open area for this one. Plays well with 12 to 25 (or more) for 15 to 20 minutes.

Process: This is a very active version of, Rock, Paper, Scissors (RPS). If you don't know about RPS you can ask around – within five inquiries you will find someone who knows how to play. In Egg-olution everyone starts as an "Egg" in a squatting down position and moves around in a duck walk. Players waddle up to someone else in the squatting position and play RPS. Whoever wins "evolves" into a "Baby Chick" – standing with hands on hips flapping their little wings. The loser (second place) remains an Egg to waddle off some more in search of another Egg - in hopes to evolve after a RPS win. Baby Chicks go up to other Baby Chicks to play RPS. Losses at the Baby Chick level go back to being an Egg. Winners at the Baby Chick level become a "Strutting Rooster" – moving around with thumbs under armpits flapping the wings and "strutting" the head back and forth. Strutting Roosters look for other Roosters to RPS. Rooster losers go back down to Baby Chicks. Winning Rosters become "Enlightened Beings" - standing still with arms crossed looking very.....enlightened. Enlightened beings can RPS with anyone, but never "devolve" back down,

they just help others "egg-volve"!!

Singing Con-Science (found in *Cooking with Play 4 Peace*) You just need some sitting around area. Works well with 12 to 25 for 15 to 25 minutes.

Process: (Just a quick plug – *Cooking for Play 4 Peace* is a wonderful activity booklet designed to promote peaceful and playful community building. We highly recommend it. See the Resources section for more information.) Have one or two players leave the room – somewhere they cannot hear the rest of the group. With the rest of the group, choose a word that you will want the absent player(s) to try and figure out – a word with two or more syllables. Initially we start out with a two-syllable word and work our way up to the longer ones. So, a word like Teamwork is pretty easy to start with. The idea here is that half of the group is going to repeat the word "team" and the other half is going to repeat the word "work" – everyone in the group saying their word at the same time - until the player(s) sent from the room guess the word. To play the absent player(s) is (are) asked to return to the group. On the count of "1, 2, 3," the players start saying their word. The guesser shouts out the full word when he believes he has it. If it's not the word players continue their chant until he gets it. Do a few two-letter words then move up to Leadership, Sportsmanship, Community, Cooperation (hard one), Whatchamakallit (a great candy bar!), etc.

We're a... They're a... You'll need a nice open space for this one. Plays well with 12 to 24 players for 20 to 30 minutes.

Process: We're A...They're A... is a great lead-in to Speed Rabbit and other Worldly Things found below (but you can use it as a stand alone as well). You'll find it best to split your group into small teams of 3 players (we have worked it out when there are 4

in a group by having players switch out with each other every round). It plays somewhat like charades. You'll give all the groups two minutes to create one (and maybe a backup) three-person life size caricature of something – common caricatures have included a grove of trees swaying in the wind, an elephant with big ears, two lumber jacks cutting down a tree, an outhouse roof over a sitter, tall grass blowing in the wind, a jump-roper (see picture) and so on. The overall objective here is that the group will be choosing three of the best life-size caricatures to use in a game of Speed Rabbit and Other Worldly Things (at least that's what we use it for). After the allotted time the game can begin. One at a time the groups will display their caricature to the rest of the players. The first player to guess what the caricature is wins a point for their team – the facilitator gets to be the judge so she will need to know what the group is going to present before they do so. After the first round give the players another two minutes to create another caricature for the second round. The energy is usually pretty good for three or four rounds. After the last round decide as a group what three caricatures they want to use in Speed Rabbit and Other Worldly Things. **Variations:** Another one of Chris' favorites is doing this one with Foam Noodles included in the caricature – great visuals!

Speed Rabbit and Other Worldly Things

(a.k.a., Elephant, Palm Tree, Monkey from the New Games Foundation) You'll need a mid-size open area. Plays well with 12 to 25 for 15 to 25 minutes.

Process: Have the group form a Double Chicken Wing circle (see The Chicken Game in Frontloaders) around you. Show them two or three caricatures they will be using during the game like the ones described in We're a…They're a…above (or of course do a quick practice of the ones the group chose to use after playing We're a…They're a…). What you will be doing (as the facilitator) is standing inside the circle and pointing to someone stating a carica-ture like, "Lumberjacks!" and then counting to 5 (or higher if you want to make it a bit easier). The player you point at brings his arms up as the tree and the two players to either side of him start chopping motions at his legs. Or you might ask them to do the famous "elephant" pose. The person you point to holds out an extended arm from the vicinity of their nose wrapping the other arm up around the first and pinching the nose with the fingers to form the trunk of the elephant. The two players on either side use their arms to form a "C" placing them near the head of the player pointed at to represents the ears of the elephant. If a player does not make the appropriate part of the caricature, within the count of 5 (or whatever number), then this person takes the place of the player in the middle – this new player now points and calls out one of the three caricatures chosen for the game. As a facilitator you might want to do a few practice rounds staying in the middle so the group understands how to play. Then let them know when the practice is over and the counting begins. When the energy starts to fade a facilitator can jump into the center of the circle as well – now two players are pointing.

"Call Us" if you have questions!
Be well and happy out there. Why not?

Challenge Energizers

This section includes a number of no-prop "fast-and-furi-ous" group challenges. Some of the challenges are timed events (again, if you borrow a wrist watch for timing is it still a no-prop activity?) – what will your groups World Record be? Some of them are "just-to-see-if-they-can-do-it" types. Keep them in this format and have the group pick a number they want to try, or cut and paste them on to index cards and have someone, "pick a card, any card." The intention here is fun and challenge (and maybe even to fill some time). If the challenge stalls, take a timeout, maybe try another challenge and come back to the stall later.

1. Line up in a circle in alphabetical order, by first names, without talking.

2. Line up in alphabetical order by last names with your eyes closed.

3. Get in groups of people who share the same favorite color without vocal sounds.

4. Get into groups of people who share the same favorite food without talking.

5. Say the alphabet backwards, starting from Z, ending with A, in under _____ sec.

6. Using one letter from each person's name (first or last), create a proper sentence – punctuation is free. (Groups of less than 10 can use two letters each.)

7. Spell the word "TEAMWORK" using your bodies as the letters.

8. In under 4 minutes, create each letter of the alphabet, in order from A to Z, using your bodies to make the letters.

9. Pass a "High Five" clap around your group - each player giving and getting, one clap at a time in under _____ seconds. (About 1 second/player.)

10. Choose five players to name all the people in the group. (If there are over 15 people in the group, have three players name them all. If there are over 25 pick another challenge card to play.)

11. How many hands can your group put together where each hand is touching every other hand?

12. Circle up the group. All players are asked to touch feet to feet at the sides. Now ask the group to move around the circle (half way or all the way) without breaking any feet-to-feet contact.

13. Stack as many fists vertically on top of each other without any player leaving the ground.

14. As a group, link together in a circle making each link in between players different.

15. Number your group 1 to ?? Now line up in alphabetical order based on the spelling of the number each player has – as quickly as possible.

16. Stack flat hands on top of each other palms down. Now, reverse the order of hands as quickly as possible keeping palms down at all times.

17. Say your names (each player saying there own) in "order" as fast as humanly possible.

18. Make the longest continuous sound – one player at a time. Each player may only sound one time.

19. Make the fewest possible points of contact with the ground using all the members of your group – no other resources allowed.

20. Choose two team members to make a "hole" by holding hands. Position the hole for optimal success (then it becomes stationary). The rest of the team has to go through the hole without touching any part of the "hole makers" (the two team members). Restart after a touch.

21. USe your fingers (everyone needs to be included), come up with a math formula that equals_____. (Any number can be used.)

add your own challenge energizers....

Lateral Challenges

Lateral Challenges are short story conundrums you (or someone else) tell the group. After hearing the story the group tries to solve the riddle by asking the teller questions that can be answered with either a "yes" or "no" response (another possible answer is "doesn't matter"). These Lateral Challenges are good for developing listening skills, formulating questions, and deductive reasoning - and they are also fun. We use them during sit down times, breaks, walking from place-to-place, and sometimes for time fillers. (*Google* Paul Sloane for additional Lateral Puzzle resources.) FYI: The * indicates riddles that have a deeper meaning you might want to talk about after.

1. Early one Sunday morning in the mansion of Sir. Edward Collumstocker, it was discovered that one of Sir Edward's precious chocolate éclairs was missing. Only three people were in the house that morning. The Maid claims she was making the beds upstairs. The Butler said he was out getting the mail and the cook was out gathering eggs from the chickens. Who Dunit? *No mail is delivered on Sunday – the Butler did it!*

2. *A young woman lives on the 12th floor of an apartment building. Every day she takes the elevator down to the first floor to go off to work. Every day, when she returns, she rides the elevator to the 6th floor and then takes the stairs the remaining six floors – unless it's raining, then she takes the elevator all the way to the 12th floor. Why? *The woman is a dwarf. She is too short to press any elevator buttons higher than the 6th floor. When it's raining, she carries her umbrella so she uses this to press the 12th floor button.*

3. Two neighbors were talking over the fence when it started to rain. The one neighbor said to the other, "You're a lucky man, your lawn always gets more rain than mine." Why is this true? *The one neighbor has more land than the other.*

4. A skilled gemologist is having difficulty handling a diamond. Why? *He is on a black diamond (difficult) ski run.*

5. It is 8 pm and Billy turns on the television to watch his   favorite show. It is an hour-long program, but he only   watches it until 8:45 and then turns off the television. He watches the show in this manner each week – never missing an episode and is always able to tell you how the show ends. How is this possible? *He tapes the show earlier in the day and fast forwards through the commercials.*

6. A man and his wife played five games of backgammon in there living room one evening. There were no draws in any of the games, yet each won the same number of games and lost the same number of games. How could this happen? *They were not playing each other.*

7. A man bought a parrot from the local pet store that was guaranteed to repeat every word it heard. When the man brought the parrot home, the parrot did not utter a single work spoken to it. Why? *The parrot was deaf.*

8. One morning a woman was cleaning her house when she accidentally knocked the pie, that had been cooling on the sill, out the window. When she looked out the window, it is nowhere to be found. Why? *The woman lives on a houseboat.*

9. A karate expert breaks a bone. He is not in any pain, but is disappointed. His friend cries out happily. Why? *The karate expert broke off the short end of a wishbone from a chicken.*

10. When Charlie Walker joined the Hallonton Police Department, his picture was on the front page of the town's paper. All the officers liked him, and he was on some of the biggest cases the department had. When Charlie finally retired from the force he did not receive any retirement benefits or the traditional gold watch from the Department. Why? *Charlie was a police dog.*

11. Two monkeys were lying next to each other one evening. By the next morning the two had disappeared, yet they did not climb, walk, or run away. What happened? *The monkeys were animal crackers – someone ate them.*

12. *An old man with epilepsy starts shaking uncontrollably, and falls to the ground. Even though his son knows the situation is serious, he does not call for medical assistance, nor does he offer any. Why? *The two men are experiencing an earthquake.*

13. *A couple has two sons who were born in the same hour of the same day in the same year, but they were not twins. Why? *The boys were part of a set of triplets, they have a sister.*

14. After a long day at work a man walks into a bar and falls immediately unconscious. Why? *The man walked into a low-hanging iron bar and knocked himself out.*

15. David, Scott, and Jimmy Turner all jump into Mr. Turner's Pickup truck after attending a local football game. Mr. Turner pulls into his driveway, where he, David, and Scott leave the truck and enter the house. Jimmy leaves the truck as well, waves goodbye, and heads down the street. Where is he going? *He's going home. He is a friend of David and Scott who just happens to share the same last name.*

16. *A woman stood looking through the window on the tenth floor of an office building. Suddenly, she was overcome by an urge and opened the window and jumped through it. It was a sheer drop outside the building to the ground, yet she was completely unhurt when she landed. Why? *The female window washer jumped from the outside to the inside of the building so she could go to the bathroom – to satisfy her urge to "go."*

17. Kimberly threw a ball as hard and as far as she could. The ball did not hit the ground, nor did it hit any walls, yet it immediately returned to her. How? *She threw the ball straight up in the air.*

18. *Mr. Wallace was a prosperous investor. He made over a million dollars a year investing in stocks. However, he never paid a cent of income tax to the U.S. government. Why? *Mr. Wallace is a Canadian citizen.*

19. *Five men were going down a country road together when it started to rain. Four of the men began to walk faster, but the fifth man made no effort to speed up. However, he remained dry while the other four got wet. They all arrived at their destination together. How? *The four men were carrying a coffin with the fifth man inside.*

20. *A mother takes her small child to have her ears pierced. The mother decides that she would like to get hers pierced as well. However, the attendant states he cannot pierce the mother's ears. Why? *The mother is under 18 – she needs her mother's permission.*

21. A man takes a watch up to the sales counter and the woman behind the counter says, "$200." Two hundred dollars are exchanged and the man leaves the shop without the watch. He never goes back. Why? *The shop is a pawnshop where the man received $200 for a watch he brought in.*

22. *Two men break into a local business, setting off the alarms. They quickly take as many valuables as they can and run back outside where they find themselves face-to-face with a swarm of police officers and the business owner. The two men hand over all the valuables to the business owner and are never arrested. Why? *The two men are fireman who were able to save some of the business owners' valuable merchandise.*

23. Cindy buys a new pair of shoes specifically for her upcoming vacation. On the day she leaves, she does not bother packing them, nor does she ever put them on during her vacation. Why? *They are brake shoes for her car.*

24. *A nervous, shifty-eyed man steps on the train. No one notices him except a woman who gives him a questioning look. He immediately gets off the train. Why? *The man is stepping on her wedding train.*

25. *John had been a stock salesman for 15 years. He was aware of the rules against insider trading, yet he bought stock from a friend's company after the friend confided in him about the impending good fortune of the company. The government knew of his actions, but did nothing. Why? *He bought livestock.*

26. A distraught woman is sitting in a bar frantically search-ing for her lost key. She knows that if she can't find the key she will lose her job. Why? *She is a singer.*

27. *A man driving through town was clocked by the police going 25 miles and hour in a 30 mile an hour zone. The police pulled the man over for passing cars that were going 30 miles and hour. Why? *The man was going the wrong way on a one-way street.*

28. A main wire going over a bridge in Boston snaps. The bridge is located within the Boston City limits. It is replaced immediately, but the taxpayers of Boston do not pay a penny for the replacement. Why? *It is a guitar string and bridge.*

29. A young lady suddenly opens the door and steps out of a car traveling 50 mph yet she is not injured. Why? *She is mov-ing from one car to the next on a train.*

30. Ingrid lives in the Swiss Alps. One December morning, she decides to go skiing. It is 2 degrees Celsius outside in the Alps, but she does not wear a coat, hat, or gloves. Why? *She is on vacation in a warm location – she is not in the Alps - and decides to go water skiing.*

Resource Information

Manual References

Karl Rohnke - You can find Karl's books (one of the founding fathers of adventure-based activities) at: **www.kendallhunt.com** You can also call them at: 1-800-228-0810 and ask them for their "Hands-On Learning" catalog filled with adventure-based books. You can also visit Karl at: www.karlrohnke.com

Sam Sikes - You can find Sam's books (a creative icon in my opinion) at his site: **www.doingworks.com** Sam has activity books and resources specifically geared towards adventure-based adult programming.

Jim Cain - You can find Jim's award winning book, _"Teamwork and Teamplay_ " and Jim's latest activity book using lengths of Webbing, _"The Book on Raccoon Circles"_ at Jim's outstanding website at:
  www.teamworkandteamplay.com His site includes useful adventure-based resources and Jim's available trainings.

Mike Spiller - Contact Mike for information on his Games of the World workshops and booklets of games covering a wide variety of topics from "Games for Small Spaces" to "Games for the Playground" (over 25 different booklets available). Email Mike at: msgow@houston.rr.com or visit www.physiciansofphun.com Mike is the best game resource I know!

Laurie Frank - Order your copy of, _"The Caring Classroom: Using Adventure to Creatre Community in the Classroom and Beyond"_ from your local bookstore - ISBN# 0-8251-9990-5. Or call Wood N Barnes Publishing at 800-678-0621. We highly recommend this book..

Neil Mercer - Tuval Organisational Effectiveness. Tuval D. N. Bik'at Bethakeren, 25166 Israel.   tuvalseminar@canaan.co.il

Faith Evans - co-author of *"99 of the best Experiential Corporate Games we know"* and *"The more the merrier: Activities for large groups."* Faith is the owner of PlayFully specializing in training and development to catalyze life changing growth. You can contact her by email: faithevans@aol.com

Michelle Cummings - owner of *Training Wheels* - your source for teambuilding kits on wheels and a wide variety of Processing/Reviewing tools. www.training-wheels.com

Sean McFeely - seanm@worldimpact.org

Patrick Gallagher - patrick@corpadventures.com

"Cooking for Play for Peace" - This wonderful book was put together by Hal Kuczwara and Craig H. Dobkin. For a donation to Play for Peace Denver you can get yourself a copy. Contact them at (720) 317-3167.

"Reflective Learning: Theory and Practice" by Sugerman, Doherty, Garvey and Gass. This book is filled with activities that help you process adventure-based activities. ISBN# 0-7872-6561-6

"No Supplies Required" by Dan McGill. Dan says, 95 ready-to go games...all you need are teenagers [they work great with other ages too]. ISBN# 1-55945-700-7

"The New Games Book" and *"More New Games"* by The New Games Foundation. ISBN#s 0-385-12516-X and 0-385-17514-0

"Are you more like: 1001 colorful quandaries for quality conversations" by Chris Cavert & Susana Acosta. Find it, and other pocket prompters, at the www.fundoing.com website store.

Additional Resources

Tom Heck - Be sure to check Tom's Teach Me Teamwork web-site: www.teachmeteamwork.com   His site is loaded with teambuilding resources - even streaming video!

Roger Greenaway - Check out the best reviewing/processing web-site on the planet!! **www.reviewing.co.uk** (don't pass this one up!!!)

Recommended Readings

"Back Pocket Adventures" by Karl Rohnke & Jim Grout. 34 more no-prop adventure-based activities from two other great guys! ISBN# 0-536-01419-1.

"The Game and Play Leader's Handbook: Facilitating Fun and Positive Interaction" by Bill Michaelis & John M. O'Connell. We highly recommend game leaders to get this book. ISBN# 1-892132-02-8

"Processing the Experience: Strategies to Enhance and Generalize Learning" second edition, by John L. Luckner & Reldan S. Nadler. Theory book on processing and working with groups. ISBN# 0-7872-1000-5

"The Theory of Experiential Education" edited by Warren, Sakofs & Hunt (the last edition I have is the 3rd). This book is a collection of articles addressing the historical, philosophical, social, and psychological foundations of Experiential Education. ISBN# 0-7872-0262-2 or buy direct from AEE at www.aee.org

Adventure-Based Training Providers

Chris Cavert - offers a wide variety of adventure-based activity trainings. Check the Trainings page at:www.fundoing.com

Dick Hammond - provides leadership and teambuilding experiences as well as challenge course skills training programs. You can email: dick@leadershiponthemove.com

Leahy & Associates - offers some great trainings. Tom also hosts the National Challenge Course Practitioners Symposium every year attended by a host of adventure-based practitioners. Information is available at: www.leahy-inc.com

Learning Unlimited - offers a number of adventure-based activities and skills trainings throughout the year. Check them out at: www.learningunlimited.com

About the Authors

Dick Hammond is the owner of the experiential leadership development company, *Leadership on the Move*. For more than a decade, Dick has worked with hundreds of corporate and non-profit organizations. He has facilitated interactive leadership workshops for fortune 500 companies such as American Airlines and Verizon Communications and small "Mom & Pop"

businesses across the country. His work with the not-for-profit sector and the community based leadership programs are an especially rewarding part of Dick's commitment to leadership skills training. Dick is a firm believer in using interactive initiatives to teach leadership skills, communication, trust and all aspects of team building needed to develop and maintain a successful organization.

Chris Cavert has been playing (less afraid than his picture) for over 42 years now - and getting payed for it the last 26. To date, Chris has had the opportunity to publish 10 adventure-based activity related books - several he co-authored with some remarkable individuals. Chris is the owner and operator of FUNdoing - an adventure-based training and resource provider. He has presented workshops at many different conferences around the country including the Asso-

ciation for Experiential Education International and regional conferences, the National Challenge Course Practitioners Symposium, and the International Drop-Out Prevention Conference. Chris truly believes that the purposeful use of adventure-based activities can really make a difference in the lives of the young (and not-so-young) people in this world.

Chris and Dick are both available for workshops and trainings.

Have fun! Be well!